ACADEMIC ENCOUNTERS

AMERICAN STUDIES

Reading
Study Skills
Writing

Jessica Williams

Intermediate

CAMBRIDGE
UNIVERSITY PRESS

CAMBRIDGE UNIVERSITY PRESS
Cambridge, New York, Melbourne, Madrid, Cape Town, Singapore, São Paulo, Delhi

Cambridge University Press
32 Avenue of the Americas, New York, NY 10013–2473, USA

www.cambridge.org
Information on this title: www.cambridge.org/9780521673709

© Cambridge University Press 2008

First published 2008
2nd printing 2008

Printed in the United States of America

A catalog record for this publication is available from the British Library

ISBN 978-0-521-67370-9 paperback

Cover and book design: Adventure House, NYC
Text composition: TSI Graphics

ACADEMIC ENCOUNTERS

The *Academic Encounters* series uses a sustained-content approach to teach students the skills they need to be successful in academic courses. There are two books in the series for each content focus: an *Academic Encounters* title and an *Academic Listening Encounters* title. Please consult your catalog or contact your local sales representative for a current list of available titles.

Titles in the *Academic Encounters* series at publication:

Content Focus and Level	Components	*Academic Encounters*	*Academic Listening Encounters*
HUMAN BEHAVIOR High Intermediate to Low Advanced	Student's Book Teacher's Manual Class Audio Cassettes Class Audio CDs	ISBN 978-0-521-47658-4 ISBN 978-0-521-47660-7	ISBN 978-0-521-60620-2 ISBN 978-0-521-57820-2 ISBN 978-0-521-57819-6 ISBN 978-0-521-78357-6
LIFE IN SOCIETY Intermediate to High Intermediate	Student's Book Teacher's Manual Class Audio Cassettes Class Audio CDs	ISBN 978-0-521-66616-9 ISBN 978-0-521-66613-8	ISBN 978-0-521-75483-5 ISBN 978-0-521-75484-2 ISBN 978-0-521-75485-9 ISBN 978-0-521-75486-6
AMERICAN STUDIES Intermediate	Student's Book Teacher's Manual Class Audio CDs	ISBN 978-0-521-67369-3 ISBN 978-0-521-67370-9	ISBN 978-0-521-68432-3 ISBN 978-0-521-68434-7 ISBN 978-0-521-68433-0

2-Book Sets are available at a discounted price. Each set includes one copy of the Student's Reading Book and one copy of the Student's Listening Book.

Academic Encounters:
Human Behavior 2-Book Set
ISBN 978-0-521-89165-3

Academic Encounters:
Life in Society 2-Book Set
ISBN 978-0-521-54670-6

Academic Encounters:
American Studies 2-Book Set
ISBN 978-0-521-71013-8

Introduction

This Teacher's Manual provides:

- information about *Academic Encounters: American Studies* (page vi)

- a brief description of the *Academic Encounters* series (page vii)

- an overview of *Academic Encounters* Reading, Study Skills, and Writing books (page vii)

- general teaching guidelines for *Academic Encounters: American Studies* (page ix)

- specific teaching instructions for *Academic Encounters: American Studies* and answers for the tasks (page 1)

- photocopiable unit quizzes with answers for *Academic Encounters: American Studies* (page 94)

ABOUT *ACADEMIC ENCOUNTERS: AMERICAN STUDIES*

Academic Encounters: American Studies is a reading, study skills, and writing text based on content taught in American history and culture courses in high schools, colleges, and universities in the United States. In this book, authentic materials have been used as the basis for texts that use academic content and style in such a way as to be accessible to intermediate students.*

New Features in *Academic Encounters: American Studies*

- **More emphasis on vocabulary skills**
  More vocabulary tasks are included. Many key terms are defined within the context of the readings, and students are taught how to recognize these embedded definitions. Students are also instructed in organizing and maintaining a vocabulary notebook.

- **More emphasis on writing skills**
  In addition to tasks in which students answer test questions, complete sentences, and write their own original sentences, a two-page writing section is presented at the end of each chapter. It provides students with an opportunity to use their academic writing skills in an assignment related to the content of the chapter or unit. Students are guided from the preparing-to-write stage through the actual writing, and they are then introduced to post-writing analysis and revision.

---

* Note that although the term *Americas* can be used to refer to all of North and South America, *America* is often used to refer to the United States of America alone. The phrase "American Studies" in the title of this book reflects that usage. "American Studies" is an academic discipline with a focus similar to that of this book: United States history and culture.

- **More emphasis on note-taking skills**

  Students are taught to take notes in several ways. They are also taught ways to check the accuracy of their notes and ways to use their notes to prepare for tests and writing assignments.

Correlation with Standards

Academic Encounters: American Studies introduces students to many of the topics and skills in the United States secondary school standards for American history and social studies. For more information about the standards, go to www.cambridge.org/us/esl/academicencounters.

TOEFL® iBT Skills

Many of the tasks in *Academic Encounters: American Studies* (as well as those in all *Academic Encounters* books) teach academic skills tested on the TOEFL® iBT test. For a complete list of the tasks taught, see the Task Index on page 241 of the Student's Book.

ABOUT THE *ACADEMIC ENCOUNTERS* SERIES

This content-based series is for students who need to improve their academic skills for further study. The series consists of *Academic Encounters* books that help students improve their reading, study skills, and writing, and *Academic Listening Encounters* books that help students improve their listening, note-taking, and discussion skills. Each reading book corresponds in theme to a listening book, and each pair of theme-linked books focuses on a subject commonly taught in academic courses. For example, *Academic Encounters: American Studies* and *Academic Listening Encounters: American Studies* focus on topics in American history and culture; *Academic Encounters: Life in Society* and *Academic Listening Encounters: Life in Society* focus on sociology; and *Academic Encounters: Human Behavior* and *Academic Listening Encounters: Human Behavior* focus on psychology and human communications. A reading book and a listening book with the same content focus may be used together to teach a complete four-skills course in English for Academic Purposes.

OVERVIEW OF *ACADEMIC ENCOUNTERS* READING, STUDY SKILLS, AND WRITING BOOKS

The approach

Academic Encounters adopts a content-based approach to the study of academic English. Students read through the texts seemingly with the prime purpose of understanding the content. In fact, as students work with the text by doing the accompanying tasks, they are also learning reading skills, study skills, and test-preparation strategies. Additionally, the texts are used for language study, so students become familiar with the vocabulary and sentence structures used in academic discourse.

Each unit of an *Academic Encounters* book focuses on some aspect of the book's content focus. The fact that the book has a unified thematic content throughout has several advantages. First, it gives students a realistic sense of studying in an academic course, in which each week's assignments are related to and build on each other. Second, as language and concepts recur, students begin to feel that the texts are getting easier, which helps to build their confidence as readers of academic text. Finally, after completing the book, some students may feel that they have enough background in the content focus area to take a course in that subject (for example, American history or an aspect of American culture) to fulfill part of their general education requirements.

In the high-intermediate to advanced reading books, students are presented with authentic samples of academic text. The material has been abridged and occasionally reorganized, but on the sentence level, little of the language has been changed. In *Academic Encounters: American Studies*, authentic materials have been used as the basis for texts that use academic content and style that is accessible to intermediate students. In all the Reading, Study Skills, and Writing books, students use the texts to develop their reading and study skills, and the high-interest content of the texts provides stimulus for writing assignments.

The content

The topics and texts in each chapter were chosen both for their importance to the theme of the book and for their appeal to students. It is important for students to be interested in what they are reading about and studying, and for them to be able to make personal connections to it. According to language acquisition theory, language development occurs more readily under such conditions. Similarly, it can be argued that the writing process is facilitated when students are well informed on a topic, have developed personal connections to it, and are engaged by it.

The skills

The main goal of the *Academic Encounters* Reading, Study Skills, and Writing books is to give students the skills and the confidence to approach an academic text, read it efficiently and critically, and take notes that extract the main ideas and key details. But the goal of academic reading is not just to retrieve information. It is also important for a student to be able to display that knowledge in a writing assignment or test-taking situation. For this reason, tasks that develop test-preparation and writing skills appear throughout the books. A longer writing assignment is at the end of each chapter.

Student interaction

Although the *Academic Encounters* Reading, Study Skills, and Writing books are centered on these skills, speaking activities abound. Students discuss the content of the texts before and after reading them; they often work collaboratively to solve task problems; they perform role-play activities; and they frequently compare answers in pairs or small groups.

Order of units

In terms of reading topics and vocabulary, the order of units is regarded as optimal. In addition, tasks build upon each other so that, for example, a note-taking task later in the book may draw upon information that has been offered in an earlier unit. Teachers who want to teach the units out of order, however, may do so. They can use the Task Index at the back of the Student's Book to see what types of tasks have been presented in earlier units and build information from those tasks into their lessons.

Course length

Each of the five units of a Reading, Study Skills, and Writing book contains a unit preview section and eight readings, and represents approximately 16–20 hours of classroom material. An *Academic Encounters* book could thus be a suitable course book for a 64- to 80-hour course (when a teacher selects four of the five units) or an 80- to 100-hour course (when all the units are used). The course can, however, be made shorter or longer. To shorten the course, teachers might choose not to do every task in the book and to assign some tasks and texts as homework, rather than do them in class. To lengthen the course, teachers might choose to supplement the book with some content-related material from their own files and to spend more time developing students' writing skills.

Task pages and text pages

Task pages are clearly differentiated from text pages by a colored vertical bar that runs along the outside edge of the page. The text pages have been designed to look like standard textbook pages. The text is in a column that takes up only two-thirds of the page, thus allowing space in the margins for glossed terms and illustrations. Figures, tables, and boxed inserts with additional information related to the topic are also included on text pages, as they are in standard textbooks. This authentic look helps to create a sense for students that they are actually reading from an academic textbook.

Task commentary boxes and task index

When a task type occurs for the first time in the book, it is headed by a colored commentary box that explains what skill is being practiced and why it is important. When the task occurs again later in the book, it may be accompanied by another commentary box, as a reminder or to present new information about the skill. At the back of the book, there is an alphabetized index of all the tasks. Page references in boldface indicate tasks that are headed by commentary boxes.

GENERAL TEACHING GUIDELINES FOR *ACADEMIC ENCOUNTERS: AMERICAN STUDIES*

Each of the five units is organized as follows:

- a unit title page
- a Previewing the unit page
- a Unit contents page

- two chapters, each of which contains four readings with accompanying tasks

- a unit content quiz (photocopiable pages in this Teacher's Manual)

Each of the ten chapters is divided into the following sections:

- Preparing to read

- Now read

- After you read

- Writing assignment

The remainder of this section contains general teaching guidelines for each element. See pages 1–93 of this Teacher's Manual for more detailed information, specific ideas for teaching each text and task, and answers to the tasks.

Unit title page

Each unit title page contains the title of the unit, a large illustration or photograph that is suggestive of the content of the unit, and a brief paragraph that summarizes the unit. This page is intended to look like a typical unit opening page in an academic course book.

Look at the title of the unit with students and make sure they understand what it means. Then look at the picture and have students describe it and attempt to relate it to the title. Help them with vocabulary as necessary.

Finally, look at the summary paragraph at the bottom of the page. Read it with your students and check to be sure that they understand the vocabulary and key concepts. At this point, it is not necessary to introduce the unit topics in any depth, since the unit preview activities that follow will achieve this goal.

Previewing the unit

Following the unit title page is a two-page spread that includes, on the right-hand side, a contents page listing the titles of the two chapters in the unit and the titles of the four texts in each chapter. This unit contents page resembles the typical chapter or unit contents page of an academic textbook. On the left-hand page of the spread are tasks that relate to the titles on the unit contents page. These tasks preview the unit either by having students predict what information might be found in each section or by giving them some information from the unit and having them respond to it. In this way, students are given an overview of the unit before they start reading it in order to generate interest in its content. Furthermore, students are taught the important reading strategy of previewing the titles and headings of long readings.

The unit preview activities should take about one hour of class time.

Preparing to read

In this book, prereading is regarded as a crucial step in the reading process. Prereading activities serve three main functions:

1 They familiarize students with the content of the reading, arousing their interest and activating any prior knowledge of the topic.

2 They introduce students to reading attack strategies, giving them tools to be used when they undertake future reading assignments.

3 They expose students to some of the language in the text – both the structures and the vocabulary – making the text easier to process when they actually read it.

Each page of prereading tasks should take approximately 20 minutes of class time. Some may require more or less time.

Although one or two prereading tasks are always included for each text, you should look for ways to supplement these tasks with additional prereading activities. As you and your students work through the book, students become exposed to more and more prereading strategies. Having been introduced to these, students should be adding them to their repertoire, and you should encourage their regular use. For example, after having practiced the prereading strategies of examining graphic material, previewing headings, and skimming, students should ideally carry out these operations before each and every text.

In general, the lower the level of students' reading and overall language proficiency, the more important extensive prereading becomes. The more prereading tasks they undertake, the easier it is for students to access the text when it comes time for them to do a closer reading.

Now read

At the bottom of each "Preparing to read" page is an instruction that tells students to read the text. This is a deceptively simple instruction that raises an important question: How closely should students read the text at this point? Some students, after doing prereading tasks, believe that now they should read slowly and carefully. But students should be discouraged from doing this. For one thing, it is a poor use of class time to have students poring silently over a text for 20 minutes or more, and more importantly, it is vital that students begin to train themselves to read quickly, tolerating some ambiguity and going for understanding main ideas and overall text structure rather than every word and detail.

To promote faster reading, this text includes several speed-reading tasks (in Chapters 4, 7, and 10), in which students try to put into operation techniques for faster reading. If students consistently apply these techniques, most texts will take between 3 and 7 minutes to read. Before students start reading any text, therefore, it is a good idea to give them a challenging time limit, which they should aim toward to complete their reading of the text.

An alternative to reading every text in class is to assign some of the longer texts as homework. When you do this, you should do the prereading tasks in class at the end of the lesson and then start the next class by having students quickly skim the text before moving on to the "After you read" tasks.

After you read

These tasks are of many different types and serve several different functions. You should not expect to find many conventional reading comprehension tasks. Instead, students are often asked to demonstrate their understanding of a text in less direct ways, such as vocabulary comprehension, language focus, study skills, and test-preparation tasks. Each task is intended as an opportunity to develop a skill, not simply to test comprehension.

Postreading tasks serve the following main functions:

1 They have students read for meaning, look for main ideas, think critically about the text, or look for inferences.

2 They ask students to think about the content, find a personal connection to it, or apply new information in some way.

3 They highlight some of the most salient language in the text, either vocabulary or grammatical structures, and have students use that language in some way.

4 They develop students' study skills repertoire by teaching them, for example, how to highlight a text, take notes, and summarize.

5 They develop students' test-preparation skills by asking them to assess what they would need to do if they were going to be tested on the text.

The end-of-chapter writing assignments

At the end of each chapter, students do an academic writing assignment based on the content of the chapter or unit. The difficulty of the assignments progresses from writing an extended definition to writing short (1- to 3-paragraph) papers. In each assignment, students are guided through the following sections:

- Preparing to write
  Students gather information on the topic, discuss and compare their information, and develop a point of view.

- Now write
  Students organize their information and write the assignment.

- After you write
  Students analyze what they have written, give and receive peer feedback, and revise if necessary.

The content quizzes

At the back of this Teacher's Manual are five content quizzes, one for each unit. Each quiz contains a mixture of true/false, multiple choice, and short-answer questions, plus one question that requires a one-paragraph answer. About 50 minutes of class time is needed to complete each quiz.

Laws of the Land

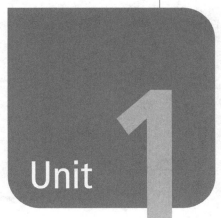

Unit title page (Student's Book pg. 1)

Make sure students understand the meaning of the unit title.
Ask them to look at the picture and think about how it relates to
the unit title.

Give students time to read the unit summary paragraph and
check to make sure they understand the areas the unit will cover.
Ask them what they know about American laws and if they know of any important
documents in American history.

Previewing the unit (Student's Book pg. 2)

Draw students' attention to the task commentary box. Discuss the importance of
previewing both for understanding the content of the unit or chapter and for
understanding its organization.

Chapter 1: The Foundations of Government

Make sure each group has decided on at least one country. If yours is a heterogeneous class,
it is usually a good idea to make sure that the members of each group are not all from the
same country. If the class is homogeneous, encourage students to consider at least one
country other than their own. The discussion need not be long, as there will be ample
opportunity to discuss these issues further throughout the chapter.

Chapter 2: Constitutional Issues Today

1 | Students should complete the true/false activity individually.

Answers

 F 1

 F 2

 T 3

 F 4

2 | An ideal group size for comparing is three to four students.

3 | You may need to give students an example to get them started. Freedom to express
your own ideas in public is one that is readily understood.

4 | Give one member of each group a chance to offer ideas. There will be plenty of
opportunities to discuss these issues in this and later units, so it need not turn into a
debate. However, you should still encourage students to support their ideas with a
few details.

Chapter 1

The Foundations of Government

1 FROM COLONIES TO UNITED STATES

Preparing to read (Student's Book pg. 4)

THINKING ABOUT THE TOPIC BEFORE YOU READ

Remind students that thinking about the topic of a text before you read it helps you to understand it better. Encourage students to do this before reading each of the texts in this book.

Ask students what they know about the early settlement of the United States by Europeans. What kinds of people arrived first? Give students time to look over the picture. Students' answers should include the ideas that the settlers are tired, perhaps sick, and that they have had a long journey. The weather is cold; it is snowy. The ship is far away; the settlers are leaving behind a familiar world and entering a new and strange one. Students should also note the presence of a Native American.

BUILDING VOCABULARY: MAKING A VOCABULARY NOTEBOOK

Building a vocabulary notebook is an important feature of the text that students will use frequently, so it is important that they understand its significance and use. Encourage them to use a separate notebook for this purpose or to create a dedicated electronic file. Model its use for the first few texts.

Now read

Refer to page xi of this Teacher's Manual for suggestions about ways in which students can read the text. You may wish to refer students to the map on page xx of the Student's Book, which shows the thirteen original colonies.

After you read (Student's Book pg. 7)

Task 1 USING HEADINGS TO REMEMBER MAIN IDEAS

Encourage students to apply this strategy throughout the text. It is very easy to use.

1 | Point out where these headings occur in the text if students have not noticed them.

2 | Students can do this activity in pairs or on their own.

Answers

<u>c</u> **1**

<u>a</u> **2**

<u>b</u> **3**

<u>a</u> **4**

<u>c</u> **5**

<u>b</u> **6**

3 | Explain why some of the items are details that do not capture the whole idea of the topic. Check students' understanding of this by asking them why, for example, 1 and 2 are not main ideas.

Answers

1 The first colonists: statement 4

2 The road to independence: statement 3

3 The United States Constitution: statement 5

Task 2 LANGUAGE FOCUS: INFINITIVES

For many of the Language Focus activities, some knowledge of grammatical terminology is required. For this task, make sure students can identify the subject of the sentence. Stress that this task focuses on sentences with two verbs.

1 | **Answers**

- "Many people from Great Britain and other countries in Europe began <u>to settle</u> in Britain's North American colonies at the end of the seventeenth century." (par. 1)
- "If you were born into a lower class, it was difficult <u>to move up</u> in the world." (par. 1)
- ". . . the settlers hoped <u>to have</u> a brighter future: <u>to buy</u> a farm, <u>to start</u> a small business, <u>to live</u> among equals." (par. 1)
- "The colonists wanted <u>to make</u> their own economic and political decisions . . ." (par. 2)
- "He wanted the colonists <u>to accept and obey</u> British laws . . ." (par. 2)
- "The king wanted the colonists <u>to pay</u> high taxes on stamps, tea, sugar, and other products." (par. 2)
- ". . . the king sent his army <u>to force</u> the colonists <u>to obey</u> . . ." (par. 2)
- ". . . colonial leaders signed the Declaration of Independence, which stated the reasons that 'the thirteen United States of America' wanted <u>to break away</u> from Great Britain." (par. 2)
- "The Americans needed <u>to make</u> some decisions . . ." (par. 3)

2 | Make sure students understand the task. As practice, ask students to complete some sentences about their own lives (e.g., I need to borrow someone's notes.).

Sample answers

1 People from Europe began to <u>come to the colonies</u>.

2 The settlers hoped to <u>start a new life</u>.

3 The army forced <u>the people</u> to <u>obey</u>.

4 The Americans needed to <u>make a decision</u>.

Task 3 LANGUAGE FOCUS: INFINITIVES OF PURPOSE

Emphasize that this is one type of infinitive. Others have different functions. The goal is for students to gain receptive and limited productive knowledge of this form.

1 | **Answer**
- "... the king sent his army <u>to force</u> the colonists to obey ..." (par. 2)
- "... a group of leaders met <u>to discuss</u> how to create a new system." (par. 4)

2 | Students may want to take notes. They will use this information in the next step.

3 | **Sample answers**

1 They came to the North American colonies to find a better life.

2 The Americans fought the British to gain independence.

3 A group of leaders met to create a new government.

Task 4 THINKING ABOUT SYMBOLS

1 | The idea of symbols should be familiar, but students may not have thought about them in this context. If you wish, you may tell them some of the stories surrounding these symbols: the crack in the Liberty Bell and the first U.S. flag. Ask if they know stories about any other American symbols (e.g., the Statue of Liberty).

2 | Give students a chance to volunteer symbols they are familiar with. Steer the discussion in the direction of national symbols (e.g., Arc de Triomphe, Niños Héroes). If they do not make the connections themselves, help them to discover that many national symbols share the themes of independence, nationalism, heroism, sovereignty, and so on. This should be a free and extended discussion.

2 A BALANCE OF POWER

Preparing to read (Student's Book pg. 9)

EXAMINING GRAPHIC MATERIAL

Discuss how previewing graphic material can help in understanding a text. The aim is not to understand the diagram on page 11 in detail at this time. Rather, students should get a general idea of the duties of the three branches of government. Tell them to focus on the lists within the boxes. This will give them a framework for understanding the text.

This task can be done individually or in pairs. At this point, students should not be concerned with the arrows between the boxes. Some of the vocabulary may be new (e.g., *enforce, impose*), but most of the verbs should be clear from the nouns that accompany them.

Answers to step 1

C 1

C 2

P 3

SC 4

C 5

P 6

C 7

P 8

Now read

Refer to page xi of this Teacher's Manual for suggestions about ways in which students can read the text.

After you read (Student's Book pg. 12)

Task 1 BUILDING VOCABULARY: CLUES THAT SIGNAL DEFINITIONS

The goals of this activity are to get students to recognize the signals of definitions that are not overt and to learn the pertinent vocabulary. Many learners are tempted to go immediately to the dictionary even when it may not be necessary.

1,2 | Call students' attention to the three signals of definitions in the excerpts. Then ask them to notice the different types of punctuation that are used.

Answers

2 veto, or block

3 override, that is, reject

3 | **Answers**

1 Congress

2 blocks

3 reject

4 | Encourage students to look back in the text if they do not know the answers immediately.

Answers

1 the highest court   **2** national   **3** constitutional

5 You may need to model or elicit one or two examples to make sure students understand the task. Answers will vary.

Task 2 UNDERSTANDING A VENN DIAGRAM

1 Make sure students understand some of the vocabulary that may be new, such as *licenses*.

2 This task can be done individually or in pairs.

Answers
F 1
T 2
T 3
T 4
F 5
F 6
T 7

Task 3 LANGUAGE FOCUS: SHOWING CONTRAST

This is a complicated topic that extends far beyond the brief explanation here. Try to avoid going into an exhaustive discussion of all the intricacies of expressing contrast. The goal is to get students to understand and to use some of the more straightforward forms that express contrast. Make sure students understand that if they change the order of the dependent and independent clause, they must change the punctuation.

1 **Answers**
- "<u>Although</u> they wanted a strong leader, they also wanted a representative government." (par. 1)
- "<u>Although</u> people often think that the President is the center of government, the Constitution lists the legislative branch first." (par. 2)
- "<u>However</u>, if Congress can gather enough votes, it can override, that is, reject, the President's veto." (par. 3)
- "<u>However</u>, both governments share certain powers." (par. 4)

2 The answers can have different subjects (e.g., the Supreme Court and Congress) or the same subject in the affirmative and negative.

Sample answers
Although the President leads the military, only Congress can declare war.
Although the President leads the military, he cannot declare war.
The President leads the military. However, only Congress can declare war.

3 Have students compare their answers in pairs.

Task 4 APPLYING WHAT YOU HAVE READ

This activity is a good check on students' understanding of the content of this chapter as well as an opportunity to use new concepts and vocabulary. If the class is large, it may be best to have the discussion in smaller groups.

3 THE BILL OF RIGHTS

Preparing to read (Student's Book pg. 15)

THINKING ABOUT THE TOPIC BEFORE YOU READ

1,2 | Students are not expected to know the answers to these items. It is simply a way to get them to start thinking about the issues addressed in this text. Some of these issues may surprise them; some may even surprise instructors. Make sure students go back to check their answers after they have read the text.

Answers
The following activities are legal in the United States. All others are unconstitutional.

2 Mr. Jones gives a speech and says that a specific group of people (for example, a racial or religious group) is the cause of many problems and should be forced to leave the United States.

6 Mr. Stone keeps a gun next to his bed at home.

8 Ms. Evans shouts at the President as he passes through a crowd. She says he is hurting the country.

Now read

Refer to page xi of this Teacher's Manual for suggestions about ways in which students can read the text. Even students unfamiliar with the information and concepts presented here may recognize Al Capone in the boxed text, but you may want to call their attention to his connection to the Constitution.

After you read (Student's Book pg. 18)

Task 1 APPLYING WHAT YOU HAVE READ

This is actually also a comprehension task, but it is straightforward and does not require inference. Understanding these three basic types of protections is crucial to students' understanding of the entire unit. Make sure this is clear before the class moves on to the next activity. This task can be done individually, but is probably best done in pairs.

1 | **Answers**

_a_	**1**	_a_	**6**
_b_	**2**	_b_	**7**
_c_	**3**	_a_	**8**
_a_	**4**	_c_	**9**
_a_	**5**		

2 | **Answers**

b 1

a 2

a 3

a 4

a 5

b 6

c 7

a 8

3 | Give students time to compare their answers.

Task 2 LANGUAGE FOCUS: VERBS OF PERMISSION

Students often think this function is limited to modal verbs. The goal of this task is to expand their repertoire to include verbs that are common in academic texts.

1 | **Answers**
- "The First Amendment does not allow anyone to say or write lies about someone that could cause harm to that person . . ." (par. 4)
- "For example, it does not allow speech that encourages people to burn down a building or kill people." (par. 4)
- "Finally, the First Amendment allows people to protest against the government if they think it is doing something wrong." (par. 4)
- "It permits them to criticize the government in speech or in writing." (par. 4)
- "The Second Amendment permits people to form a militia, or army of citizens, and to keep guns." (par. 5)
- "The Fourth Amendment forbids police searches without permission from a judge." (par. 5)
- "The Eighteenth Amendment, passed in 1919, prohibited the manufacture and sale of alcohol." (boxed text)

2 | **Answers**

1 may

2 may not

3 may

4 may not

3 | This step encourages students to process the content of the text and to use the new structures in a controlled format. You may want to do the example as a class to model the task.

Sample answers

2 The Bill of Rights permits criticism of the government.

3 The Bill of Rights does not allow speech or writing that is dangerous to others.

4 The Bill of Rights prohibits police searches without permission from a judge.

5 The Bill of Rights allows freedom of expression.

6 The Bill of Rights does not permit the publication of lies that will hurt people.

4 | This step extends the pattern introduced earlier. Because there are examples in the text, this should not be new to students.

5 | This step moves toward freer production of the new structure.

Sample answers

1 The Bill of Rights forbids the police to search without permission from a judge.

2 The Bill of Rights permits citizens to criticize the government.

3 The Bill of Rights allows citizens to express their ideas freely.

Task 3 THINKING CRITICALLY ABOUT THE TOPIC

It is expected that students will bring up topics such as the following: Criticism of the government during war may weaken the country; freedom of expression may also promote divisiveness or may allow dangerous speech; too much protection of criminal suspects may mean the guilty go free.

4 ELECTING THE PRESIDENT

Preparing to read (Student's Book pg. 20)

THINKING ABOUT THE TOPIC BEFORE YOU READ

This is an activity that students can have fun with. Make it clear that these rules apply to American citizens, so it should be obvious that citizens of other countries cannot vote no matter what their status. Students may not know what voting in the United States looks like. Point out the photo on page 23, which shows an American citizen voting. If students in your class are from different countries, you may want to ask them how voting takes place in their countries.

1 | This step can be done as a class or in small groups.

2 | It may also be helpful to make a chart encompassing all the years cited in step 1. Then students will have a handy set of criteria for disenfranchisement in the United States for the past 200 years. Encourage students to keep the chart and refer to it in subsequent tasks.

Now read

Refer to page xi of this Teacher's Manual for suggestions about ways in which students can read the text. If students are unfamiliar with the abbreviations for the states, refer them to the map on page xxi of the Student's Book.

After you read (Student's Book pg. 24)

Task 1 ASKING AND ANSWERING QUESTIONS ABOUT A TEXT

This is a strategy for active reading. Give students time to reread the text in class using this strategy. When they have finished, ask them what other questions they came up with. Then, as a class, make sure everyone can use the text to answer those questions.

Task 2 LANGUAGE FOCUS: GERUNDS

Gerunds are a relatively advanced structure but are common in academic texts. It is useful to expose learners to how gerunds are used little by little and in context.

1 | **Sample answers**

The candidates' activities during the campaign include (1) explaining their points of view to voters, (2) participating in debates, (3) advertising their campaign on television, and (4) talking about their plans for the country.

2 | **Sample answers**

1 voting

2 searching people's homes without permission

3 printing money

4 voting

Task 3 LANGUAGE FOCUS: EXPRESSING NUMERICAL DATA

These expressions are particularly prevalent in the social sciences, and students will need to use them in academic writing tasks.

1 | You may want to try a few sample sentences that draw from students' personal experiences. One possibility is to get a show of hands: How many people listened to the radio this morning? How many people had breakfast? Then have the class make up some example sentences using that information.

2 | Students may wonder about subject-verb agreement for percentages, majority, and so on. Since there is no consensus on this topic, let students express them as either singular or plural. If no one brings it up, don't mention it.

Sample answers
- Approximately 80 percent of the voting age population of Argentina, Brazil, and Australia votes in national elections.
- About 80 percent of the voting age population of Chile votes in national elections.
- More than half of the voting age population of France and Thailand votes in national elections.

3 | This can be a brief discussion.

UNIT 1 WRITING ASSIGNMENT A

Preparing to write (Student's Book pg. 26)

Definitions are a feature of academic writing but can be handled in a limited and relatively simple way with these two formats. Other formats will be introduced later in the text. The formats introduced in this section will also be recycled later.

1 | You may wish to elicit definitions in this format using more familiar content (e.g., A tiger is a . . . A banana is a . . .) before you continue. Or, if your class is heterogeneous, you may prefer to have students provide definitions for items familiar in their culture that might be unfamiliar to others (e.g., A madrassa is a . . . A durian is a . . .).

2 | This step helps students process the content from the chapter as well as practice the definition formats. You may want to do the first one together as a class.

Sample answers

1 July 4, 1776, was the day that colonial leaders signed the Declaration of Independence.

2 The Liberty Bell is a symbol of independence.

3 The Bill of Rights is a document that protects the rights of American citizens.

4 Federalism is a system of government that divides power and responsibility between the national and state governments.

5 Voter turnout is the percentage of possible voters who actually vote.

6 The Democratic Party is one of two major political parties in the United States.

3 | Go through this part of the task carefully. Be sure students understand the relationship between the XY/XYZ formats they have just produced and the more extended definition they will write in step 4.

4 | Students may want to check with you that their XY/XYZ definitions are adequate.

5 | Give students some time to complete this part of the task.

6 | This is a good time to introduce the idea of plagiarism. The ownership of ideas and words is a difficult concept for some students to grasp, and it is one that many students are unfamiliar with. It will take many reminders and lots of practice to fully understand plagiarism. It is good for learners to get into the habit of making notes for their writing assignments with the book closed. By now they should be quite familiar with the content.

Now write

Sample answer

The Bill of Rights is a document that protects the rights of American citizens. It protects the rights of individuals. It guarantees basic rights such as freedom of expression and religion. It also protects citizens against the misuse of power by the government. It guarantees fair treatment of criminal suspects by the police and in court.

After you write (Student's Book pg. 27)

Students may find it useful to see how other students have performed the same task.

Chapter 2

Constitutional Issues Today

1 FREEDOM OF EXPRESSION: HOW FAR DOES IT GO?

Preparing to read (Student's Book pg. 28)

THINKING ABOUT THE TOPIC BEFORE YOU READ

1 | Give students a few minutes to look over the pictures. They may not understand the significance of the burning cross, so this may require some explanation.

2 | This can be done as a class discussion or in small groups. Encourage students to use the suggested academic language and to consider the issues in light of what they learned in the last chapter.

Now read

Refer to page xi of this Teacher's Manual for suggestions about ways in which students can read the text. You may want to discuss the Holmes quote (boxed text, page 30 of the Student's Book) before students begin to read. It contains the main idea of this text.

After you read (Student's Book pg. 31)

Task 1 READING FOR MAIN IDEAS

This task extends the complexity of reading for main ideas in two ways. First, it holds learners accountable for their answers; that is, the task asks them to locate evidence in the text. Second, it differentiates between several important ideas and one overarching main idea.

1 │ The first steps of this task should be done individually.

   Answers

   1 par. 3

   2 par. 4

   3 par. 1

   4 par. 2

2 │ **Answer**

   2

3 │ **Answer**

   "However, the First Amendment protects even the expression of opinions that many people do not like." (par. 1)

Task 2 MAKING GENERALIZATIONS

In this task, students must *infer* the author's point regarding activities not permitted by the First Amendment, which in the text are presented by way of a series of examples. You may need to give an example:

(1) Reading a lot increases your vocabulary knowledge. (2) Reading helps with writing skills. (3) Reading a lot helps you read faster. ➤ Generalization: Reading can help you with academic work.

1,2 │ **Answer**

   They describe activities that may be harmful or dangerous.

   3 │ If this is too easy, you can ask students to create their own sentences.

   Sample answers
   • The First Amendment prohibits people from <u>expressing anything in a way that might be dangerous to others</u>.
   • <u>Dangerous speech</u> is not allowed by the First Amendment.

Task 3 BUILDING VOCABULARY: WORDS THAT CAN BE USED AS NOUNS OR VERBS

1 │ Students often find the dual function of these words confusing. After you have read these sentences, ask students if they know of other words in English that have this characteristic. They may know the ones that shift stress, such as RECord/reCORD.

2 │ **Answers**

   1 The settlers hoped for a better future.

   2 The presidential candidates debate their ideas.

3 │ If students are unfamiliar with these words, encourage them to use a dictionary. Show them where the part of speech is noted in the definition. The benefits and use of learner's dictionaries will be introduced later in the text. They are tailored to learners' needs and therefore are both easier for students to use and contain information that may not be found in other kinds of dictionaries.

Sample answers

In the early days of the colonies, the English had *control* of the government.
In the early days of the colonies, the English *controlled* the government.
The Bill of Rights includes a *guarantee* of freedom of expression.
The Bill of Rights *guarantees* freedom of expression.

Task 4 THINKING CRITICALLY ABOUT THE TOPIC

1 | These topics are not all clear-cut, which is why they are good for discussion. Encourage students to see that these issues are not always black and white and that answers may vary with the context.

Sample answers

a not if it clearly advises people to do something violent

b probably not; local laws may vary

c probably, but perhaps not if they hurt the person's reputation or livelihood

d yes

e yes

f yes, so long as it does not include suggestions for using it

g no

2 | Students' discussion should address issues of balancing freedom with safety, security, and privacy. You may have to steer them in that direction.

2 SEPARATING RELIGION AND GOVERNMENT

Preparing to read (Student's Book pg. 33)

EXAMINING GRAPHIC MATERIAL

Religion is a potentially controversial, even taboo, subject, so it is important to present it academically, much as you would any other topic. Some students may be surprised to find out that many Americans consider religion to be an important part of their lives.

1 | **Sample answer**
Religion plays an important role in the lives of many Americans.

2 | This can be done as a class discussion or in small groups.

3 | Encourage students from countries not represented on the graphs to participate. However, because this is potentially a touchy and very personal subject, don't press them if they are reluctant.

Now read

Refer to page xi of this Teacher's Manual for suggestions about ways in which students can read the text.

After you read (Student's Book pg. 35)

Task 1 READING TO FIND SUPPORT FOR MAIN IDEAS

This task extends the earlier idea of finding support for claims made in the text. In this case, the support is in the form of examples.

1 | Have students explain this idea in their own words.

2 | **Sample answers**
- "The government may not establish a church or force people to practice a particular religion or any religion at all. It may not favor or support one religion more than another." (par. 2)
- "This means that in general, religious practices and symbols are not permitted on government property, such as courts and public (government-supported) schools." (par. 2)
- ". . . teachers in public schools may not say prayers in class." (par. 2)
- "The guarantee of religious freedom in the First Amendment also means that individuals may not impose their religious beliefs on others . . ." (par. 2)

3 | **Sample answers**
- ". . . the effort to stop the march was unconstitutional because it would limit the Nazis' freedom of speech." (par. 2)
- ". . . the First Amendment protects people's right to use symbols, even burning crosses, to express their ideas." (par. 3)
- ". . . flag burning is a legal form of political protest; therefore, any law that prohibits it is unconstitutional." (par. 4)

4 | If students' answers are not similar, you may need to go over this task as a class.

Task 2 APPLYING WHAT YOU HAVE READ

This is a difficult task that requires students to draw conclusions and use the information from the text in a new context.

1, 2 | Before forming groups, you may wish to do the first few examples as a class for steps 2 and 3. Let students brainstorm for more than one solution to each of the situations that you discuss.

3 | Check that the groups are coming up with solutions that are logical, even if they are not viable. It is not important that the solutions be possible, only that students work out logical resolutions.

4 | Let each group present one solution. An interesting class discussion can develop, especially if more than one group has chosen the same conflict.

Task 3 BUILDING VOCABULARY: LEARNING VERBS WITH THEIR PREPOSITIONS

Introduce the idea of collocation – that certain words typically, though not always, appear together.

1 | This is a straightforward copying task. Students may be confused by item 3 because the preposition does not directly follow the verb.

Answers

1 with

2 in

3 on

4 with

2 | **Answers**

1 in athletic activities after school

2 on poor people

3 with the quiet and relaxing atmosphere

4 with the private lives of its citizens

3 | This final step gives most of the control to students. Try to make sure that students offer meaningful responses.

Sample answers

1 I never participate in political activities.

2 I think religion conflicts with politics.

3 People should not interfere with their friends' decisions.

Task 4 LANGUAGE FOCUS: GIVING REASONS

This topic is far more complex than the presentation here. Do not try to give it a complete treatment. This task allows students to process some of the simpler markers of causality in order to discuss the content of the chapter.

1 | You may want to do the first one as a class.

Answers

1 The authors of the Constitution included religious freedom in the First Amendment because they wanted to avoid religious conflicts.

2 The Constitution establishes a policy of "separation of church and state"; therefore, there is no national religion.

3 Because the Constitution establishes a policy of "separation of church and state," there is no national religion.

4 Since the Supreme Court has ruled that flag burning is a legal form of political protest, any law that prohibits it is unconstitutional.

2 | Make sure students give reasons provided in the text.

Sample answers

1 The government may not favor or support any particular religion; therefore, religious practices and symbols are not permitted on government property, such as schools and courts.

2 Many people left Europe for the American colonies because they wanted a better life.

3 Since the Fourth Amendment prohibits unreasonable searches, the police cannot enter a house without permission from a judge.

3 GUNS IN AMERICA: THE RIGHT TO BEAR ARMS

Preparing to read (Student's Book pg. 38)

THINKING ABOUT THE TOPIC BEFORE YOU READ

1 | Students may recall the brief mention of the Second Amendment in Chapter 1.

2 | Students' discussion should address common conceptions about guns and gun violence in the United States. Students should begin with what they already know and end with their views on gun ownership.

Now read

Refer to page xi of this Teacher's Manual for suggestions about ways in which students can read the text.

After you read (Student's Book pg. 40)

Task 1 SCANNING

Explain the difference between skimming to get a general idea of the content of a text, and scanning for specific information. Both skills are important in academic reading.

Answers

1 wild animals, hostile British soldiers

2 an army of citizens

3 broad

4 about 20 percent

Task 2 APPLYING WHAT YOU HAVE READ

1 | This text was adapted from a real newspaper article. This gives students an opportunity to understand how the Bill of Rights operates in real contexts.

2 | The probable conclusion is that in the absence of a gun, this would have remained just a fist fight, even if the young man was badly beaten.

3 | Students may want to broaden the discussion to other points.

Sample answers
- *For*: Citizens should be allowed to own guns for their own protection.
- *Against*: Guns are a major cause of violence and death.

4 | This incident seems to favor the narrow interpretation, but student opinions may differ. Don't push for a right or wrong answer. It is the application of their knowledge to a new context that is important.

Task 3 UNDERSTANDING THE FUNCTION OF TOPIC SENTENCES

Understanding topic sentences is important for reading comprehension, but it is also important for writing. This task prepares students for the writing assignments in this text. You should mention that it is not always a single sentence that fulfills this function, especially in longer texts. It is also not easy to predict whether it will be in the first, second, or final position in a paragraph. However, in this book, we advise students to place their topic sentence at the beginning of a paragraph.

1 | Encourage students to notice that some of the choices are inappropriate because they are too subjective, or they present an important detail rather than introduce the main point of the paragraph.

Answer
 F **3**

2 | **Answer**
 A **5**

3 | Knowing why other choices are not appropriate is as important as knowing why one choice is best. Students should be able to verbalize their reasons.

Sample answers

1 too specific

2 does not suggest a position

4 presents an opinion

6 presents an opinion

7 presents an opinion

8 too broad; does not suggest a position

4 | This could be a prewriting activity. With a topic sentence and several supporting points, students will have the ingredients of a paragraph.

Sample answers

For:
- Banning guns will not prevent criminals from getting guns.
- Citizens should be allowed to own guns for their own protection.
- Gun use can save lives and prevent crimes.

Against:
- Guns are a major cause of violence and death.
- Guns are often involved in accidents.
- Guns can be used against their owners.

Task 4 THINKING CRITICALLY ABOUT THE TOPIC

Students may have strong opinions about this, and now they should have the language and knowledge to form coherent arguments. This should be an open-ended discussion.

4 SECURITY VERSUS CIVIL LIBERTY

Preparing to read (Student's Book pg. 42)

REVIEWING WHAT YOU HAVE ALREADY READ

1 | By now students have read several texts with overlapping content and should be prepared to take a more critical stance. Give students some time to review the texts and their own notes. The list can be done individually or in pairs.

2 | This should be an individual activity.

3 | This can be done as a whole-class activity if the class is small but is best done in small groups.

BUILDING VOCABULARY: PREVIEWING KEY TERMS

Emphasize the importance of understanding a few key lexical items prior to reading, as opposed to understanding every word in the text.

1 | Make sure students have access to a dictionary that is adequate for the task. You may wish to introduce an online or learner's dictionary at this time. *Versus* should present little problem, but *security* and *civil liberty* may be more difficult, especially out of context. You may need to provide that for them.

Answers
security: safety; protection against attack
civil liberty: a person's right to do, think, and say what he or she wants if this does not harm other people
versus: in comparison to; against

2, 3 | Reiterate the value of prediction activities. Step 3 can be done in groups or as a whole class.

Now read

Refer to page xi of this Teacher's Manual for suggestions about ways in which students can read the text.

After you read (Student's Book pg. 44)

Task 1 INFERRING THE AUTHOR'S OPINION

Inferring is one of the most important academic reading skills, but it is also one of the most difficult. As you work through this task, point out the linguistic and other contextual cues that suggest the author's view. For example, (a) includes the phrase, "*even* if there is no evidence of a crime." Item (c) points out the secrecy of the trials, suggesting the author thinks the public *should* know. Encourage students to examine the cartoon. Cartoons are vehicles for conveying ideas that may not be expressed overtly. Remind students that there is more than one answer to some of the items.

1 | **Answers**

b	**1**
e	**2**
a, d, e	**3**
b	**4**
c	**5**

2 | This step is important since students may find this task particularly challenging and will benefit from the assistance of classmates.

3 | This can be a small-group or a class discussion. It is designed as a discussion about editorial policy and authorial prerogatives. However, students may wish to turn it into a discussion of the Patriot Act itself. This is a controversial subject, of course, so that decision must be based on the context in which you teach.

Task 2 TEST TAKING: UNDERSTANDING DIFFERENT TYPES OF TEST QUESTIONS

This is the first in a series of tasks on test-taking skills. They go from simple to more difficult. The point is to recognize the kind of questions being asked, rather than how to answer them.

1 | This can be done in pairs or individually.

Answers

1	**a**
3	**b**
1	**c**
2	**d**
2	**e**
3	**f**

2 | **Answers**

2	**a**
3	**b**
1	**c**

Type 3 questions will be more difficult to write and answer. Don't hold students to too high a standard. Subsequent tasks in this text will address how to answer such questions.

Task 3 BUILDING VOCABULARY: ORGANIZING A VOCABULARY NOTEBOOK

By now, students should have accumulated a good-sized vocabulary list, but they may need assistance organizing it. Some teachers feel new words should be grouped by topic. However, many experts in vocabulary learning claim this causes unnecessary confusion. The main goal is for students to find a system that is effective for them. If they have an established method that works for them, let them go ahead with that method.

Task 4 BUILDING VOCABULARY: REMEMBERING NEW WORDS AND PHRASES

Writing words down is important, but it is more important that students retrieve the new words frequently. This will help anchor the words in long-term memory. Retrieval can include spontaneous production, but reading, hearing, and/or privately rehearsing their use are also important.

UNIT 1 WRITING ASSIGNMENT B

Preparing to write (Student's Book pg. 47)

1 | Learners will use some of the knowledge of paragraph structure that has been introduced in this chapter. Go over this paragraph as a class. Remind students of the activities about topic sentences and supporting points in the "Guns in America" section.

2 | This can be done individually, or you can put students in small groups right away.

3 | This activity should be relatively short, as students have discussed similar topics already.

4 | Make sure students understand the two types of examples. If necessary, remind them of the ones in the example paragraph.

Now write

This is probably best done as homework. If students have prepared well in the "Preparing to Write" activities, they should be able to do this on their own. Have students refer to the sample paragraph on page 47 of the Student's Book.

After you write (Student's Book pg. 48)

Responding to the work of classmates can help learners become more aware of strengths and weaknesses in their own writing. It is important that these feedback sessions be directed and not simply address what readers liked or did not like. Each feedback session should reflect the focus of the particular writing assignment.

A Diverse Nation

Unit title page (Student's Book pg. 49)

Make sure students understand the meaning of the unit title. The word *diverse* may be unfamiliar to them in this context. Ask them to look at the photo collage and think about how it relates to the unit title. Give students time to read the unit summary paragraph and check to make sure they understand the areas that the unit will cover. Ask them what they know about the different ethnic groups in the United States, which ones are more prevalent, and the circumstances of their arrival.

Previewing the unit (Student's Book pg. 50)

Chapter 3: The Origins of Diversity

1 Students may be surprised to learn that the native population was quite large, far larger than the population of Europeans who first settled in North America. You will not be giving away too much information if you reveal the population figure of 10 million from the text. The native population on the East Coast was decimated by diseases brought by the Europeans.

2 The largest numbers of immigrants during this period were German, British, Irish, Italian, Polish, Canadian, Swedish, Norwegian, and Russian Jews.

3 This quote should introduce students to the American romance with its immigrant past. This is a theme that will run through the entire unit, so a brief discussion now will set the tone for other discussions later.

Chapter 4: Diversity in Today's United States

1 Today, the largest number of immigrants (both legal and illegal) comes from Mexico. India is a distant second, followed by other Asian countries (the Philippines, China). Students' replies should reflect their understanding of the economic pull of the United States.

2 Encourage students to refer to economic challenges and cultural differences.

3 Encourage students to refer to problems with assimilation and "fitting in."

4 This question should evoke the most thoughtful responses and the longest discussion. If the class is in the United States, students may have particular insight into cultural differences and changes across generations.

Chapter 3

The Origins of Diversity

1 AMERICA'S FIRST PEOPLE

Preparing to read (Student's Book pg. 52)

THINKING ABOUT THE TOPIC BEFORE YOU READ

1 | This question will give students a chance to air any stereotypes they have or know of regarding Native Americans. Ask them about the roles of cowboys versus Indians. Some of them may have played similar games as children. They may even have a favorite cowboy from the movies, but probably not a favorite Indian.

2 | This map is a striking illustration of what happened to native lands, and by extension, the culture of the native population. Students should be able to make accurate predictions about the content of the next text.

Now read

Refer to page xi of this Teacher's Manual for suggestions about ways in which students can read the text.

After you read (Student's Book pg. 55)

Task 1 THINKING ABOUT THE TOPIC

1 | **Sample answers**
- "Most European Americans in the eighteenth and nineteenth centuries believed that whites were superior to Native Americans." (par. 5)

- "Unfortunately, the promises in the treaties were often broken." (par. 5)

- "The government hoped that young Native Americans would learn the values and culture of white American society and give up their own traditions." (par. 7)

1 | **Sample answer**

The main reason for the conflict was that both the settlers and Native Americans wanted the same land. However, students may also make observations about the basic clash between the two cultures. Although the practical point of contention was the land, the cultural conflict was also very real, and it would be a good starting point for a brief discussion.

2 | Ask students to observe and list some of the physical differences between the two photos, such as his hair and dress, before they give a more general answer.

Sample answer

He was assimilated into white American culture.

3 | Students should draw the parallel that both the photos and maps are about change and loss: loss of land and loss of culture and identity. Students may wish to discuss this further and draw parallels with situations they know.

Task 2 APPLYING WHAT YOU HAVE READ

1 | The terrible treatment of native people is not limited to the United States. The aboriginal people of Australia and most of the colonial world are examples. Be aware that this can be a sensitive subject, for example, the Ainu people of Japan.

2 | Answers will vary. It is possible that students will not think of any examples.

Task 3 LANGUAGE FOCUS: RECOGNIZING THE PASSIVE

The passive is complex in its formation, meaning, and use, and it is not expected that students will master it during this one task. The goal is to help them to recognize when and why the passive form is used in academic writing. Stress that the use of the passive is a choice.

1 | **Answers**

1 Sometimes a tribe <u>was allowed</u> to stay on a small part of its original land.

2 Many Native-American communities <u>were</u> almost <u>destroyed</u> by the actions of the settlers and the policies of the American government.

3 The Cherokee who survived <u>were forced</u> to march 1,000 miles.

4 Traditional Indian ways <u>were replaced</u> by the customs and behavior of white Americans.

2 | This may be done as a whole class activity.

Sample answer

The focus of each sentence is on the one who experiences the action, not the thing that does the action.

3 | **Sample answers**

1 is called (P: It is not important to know who calls it the *Trail of Tears*.)

2 were imprisoned or killed (P: We don't know who imprisoned or killed them.)

3 broke (A: It is important to know who broke the treaties.)

4 were forced (P: We don't know specifically who forced them.)

5 created (A: It is important to know what created the conflict.)

2 SLAVERY: THE EARLY HISTORY OF AFRICAN AMERICANS

Preparing to read (Student's Book pg. 57)

BUILDING BACKGROUND KNOWLEDGE OF THE TOPIC

Many students know relatively little about the history of slavery and the slave trade. Pictures present some of the most graphic and affecting representations of this period.

1 Students will probably discuss the horrible conditions on a typical slave ship.

2 Explain that the term *Negro* is no longer used, and the terms *black* and *African American* are preferred today. Give examples of other contexts for auctions, such as art and livestock.

Now read

Refer to page xi of this Teacher's Manual for suggestions about ways in which students can read the text.

After you read (Student's Book pg. 60)

Task 1 USING A GRAPHIC TO SHOW A SEQUENCE OF EVENTS

1 If students had difficulty with this text, you may wish to do this step as a class.

Answers

1 Students' responses should address the fact that those involved in the Triangular Trade all depended on each other economically.

2 slaves: Africa; molasses: Caribbean; rum: northern United States; raw cotton: southern United States; cotton cloth: northern United States/Britain

3 slaves: Caribbean/southern United States; molasses: northern United States; rum: Africa; raw cotton: northern United States/Britain; cotton cloth: worldwide

2 Processing information in more than one modality helps learners to understand and remember relationships. This is especially true for visual learners.
The map should show the following relationships:
slaves: Africa ➤ Caribbean/southern United States
molasses: Caribbean ➤ northern United States
rum: northern United States ➤ Africa

Task 2 READING PRIMARY TEXTS

Slave narratives are an important source of information about this period and offer a more intimate perspective on the lives of slaves. Encourage students to visit the URL listed at the bottom of page 59 in the Student's Book to hear this narrative and to view others.

1 | Answers will vary but could include: use of dialect, oral style, personal narrative versus historical chronology and analysis.

2 | Answers will vary but should mention a more vivid sense of the personal experience of those who lived through these events.

Task 3 LANGUAGE FOCUS: RECOGNIZING THE PASSIVE IN A TEXT CHAIN

The passive is ideally suited to describe certain activities and events, in particular, multistep processes. For this part of the task, it may be useful to put the text on an overhead transparency and draw an arrow from one reference to the subsequent one. This will provide a more visual representation of the relationship among the nouns in the passage. If students have trouble getting started, you may want to identify the first key word together as a class. After they have finished, it may be useful once again to draw arrows between the key words.

Answers

Ships sailed to Caribbean ports and picked up molasses, a raw syrup made from sugar, and brought it to northern cities such as Boston and New York. The molasses was made into rum, an alcoholic drink, and then was shipped to Africa. In Africa, the rum was sold in exchange for slaves. The slaves were then shipped to the Caribbean and southern states, where they were sold, and the cycle began again.

3 A COUNTRY OF IMMIGRANTS

Preparing to read (Student's Book pg. 62)

SKIMMING

1 | Students did a scanning task in the last chapter. Emphasize that the goals of skimming are somewhat different: When a reader skims, he or she gets a general idea of the content in order to process it more easily later. Mention that skimming can also be used to determine whether a text is worth reading. For example, in doing research, students can skim a text to see if it will be a useful source.

2 | The answer should reflect the history of immigration to the United States.

THINKING ABOUT THE TOPIC BEFORE YOU READ

1 | Give students time to look over the photographs. You may also include the photographs that follow the text. Some students may have heard of or even visited

Ellis Island. You can mention that the Statue of Liberty stands in view of Ellis Island and that today, it is possible for tourists to visit both places. Ellis Island houses a museum of immigration.

2 | Answers will vary but should include the following ideas:
  1 First photo: nineteenth century; second photo: recently
  2 possibly economic opportunity or political freedom
  3 The century has changed, but the reasons for immigrating have not.
  4 Answers will vary.

Now read

Refer to page xi of this Teacher's Manual for suggestions about ways in which students can read the text.

After you read (Student's Book pg. 65)

Task 1 BUILDING VOCABULARY: USING CONTEXT

The value of inferring word meaning from context has perhaps been overemphasized. In fact, this is very difficult to do unless most of the words in the surrounding text are already known. However, it is sometimes necessary to guess the meaning of a word, so it is important to develop strategies for doing so.

1 | Some students may already know the word *persecution*. Ask them to delay giving the definition until those who do not know the word have made a guess about what it means. At the end, let them know which option was correct: that the old country did not like their religion.

2 | This may be done individually or in pairs.

Answers
  1 Many were <u>escaping</u> from a **famine** caused by the <u>failure</u> of the potato crop in Ireland. *negative*

  2 This <u>flood</u> of immigrants began to **alarm** many American citizens. They believed that the immigrants, who worked for low wages, <u>were taking their jobs away</u>. *negative*

  3 Increasingly, Americans were <u>afraid</u> that the large number of immigrants coming to the country would <u>take their jobs away</u>. Just as importantly, many American citizens believed that this large number of immigrants **threatened** the nation's identity. *negative*

  4 A new system **favored** immigrants who had relatives already living in the United States and immigrants who had <u>valuable skills</u>, particularly in engineering, science, and technology. *positive*

3 You may wish to have students share other ways they may have guessed the meaning of these words.

Task 2 NOTE TAKING: USING A CHART

1 This is the first task in a series that provides various options for note taking. Encourage students to use whichever method works best for them. Make sure students understand the three terms in step 1.

2 Make certain students understand their task: that they must fill in both times and events in the chart.

Sample answers

Time Period	Pushes	Pulls	Barriers
17th and 18th century	religious persecution in Europe	religious freedom, cheap land	expensive passage
1820–1875	economic hardship, famine	economic opportunities, gold	hostility of residents
1875–1920	economic hardship	economic opportunities	new immigration laws, quotas
after 1965	few job opportunities at home	economic opportunities, relatives living in the United States	(no barriers explained in text)

3 Give students time to compare their charts with a partner.

Task 3 THINKING ABOUT THE TOPIC

This task can be done in small groups or as a class.

1 Encourage students to see the parallels, as well as the differences, among historical and contemporary trends. They may mention economic opportunity, political freedom, and access to education.

2 Some students may think it is easier because of changes in technology, transportation, and communication. In addition, established immigrant communities may make new immigrants feel welcome. On the other hand, there may be fewer opportunities for new immigrants to "get in on the ground floor," especially those without specific and valued skills. Students may or may not know about the bureaucratic difficulties of immigrating.

3 It is a good idea to give students an opportunity to show their expertise. Students may know about patterns in their own country or another country they know well.

4 NOT ALWAYS WELCOME

Preparing to read (Student's Book pg. 67)

BUILDING BACKGROUND KNOWLEDGE OF THE TOPIC

Almost every student will be familiar with the image of the Statue of Liberty, but you might want to let them know it was a gift from the French government. Emma Lazarus wrote the poem in response to the flood of Jewish refugees who arrived in the United States following a wave of anti-Semitism and persecution in Europe.

1 | Encourage students to try to understand the poem without looking up all of the words. However, it may be helpful for you to explain a few of them; in particular, *huddled*, *yearning*, and *refuse*.

2 | The goal of these questions is to showcase the rosier side of the immigration picture: the American image of itself as a country that welcomes everyone to its shores.

3 | These questions should get students to start thinking that this rosy picture is an idealization and that, on both an individual and group basis, immigrants have often been treated with hostility.

Now read

Refer to page xi of this Teacher's Manual for suggestions about ways in which students can read the text.

➡ Remind students to review and update their vocabulary notebooks.

After you read (Student's Book pg. 70)

Task 1 HIGHLIGHTING

Make sure students look at both texts. You may wish to demonstrate one or two examples of the highlighting strategy with the text on an overhead transparency.

Sample answers

1 • "They believed that the immigrants, who worked for low wages, were taking their jobs away." ("A Country of Immigrants," par. 3)
 • "Americans were afraid that the large number of immigrants coming to the country would take their jobs away." ("A Country of Immigrants," par. 4)
 • "White workers were angry because the Chinese worked for such low wages." ("Not Always Welcome," par. 2)
 • "As with the Chinese, many Americans believed the Irish were taking away their jobs." ("Not Always Welcome," par. 3)

2 • "Some also believed that this large group of immigrants would be a problem for the rest of the population because they needed government services: schools, running water, and police protection." ("Not Always Welcome," par. 3)

3 • "Americans also found Chinese customs strange and foreign." ("Not Always Welcome," par. 2)

• "Many Americans believed that the Irish were dirty, stupid, and lazy." ("Not Always Welcome," par. 3)

• "Latin Americans, Asians, and Africans are the immigrants whose appearance and culture differ the most from the majority, that is, white Americans of European background." ("Not Always Welcome," par. 4)

Task 2 BUILDING VOCABULARY: USING A DICTIONARY

Using a dictionary effectively is an important tool in academic work. Encourage students to use a good quality learner's dictionary. Point out its advantages over other dictionaries and explain that it contains information that is not often found in dictionaries for native speakers.

1 | **Answer**

2

2 | Any or all of these could be clues to choosing the correct definition.

3 | This step could be done for homework.

Task 3 BUILDING VOCABULARY: COLLOCATIONS

Students have already been introduced to the idea of collocations in the context of verbs with prepositions. This task presents a slightly different perspective on collocations: They are expressions that typically appear with a specific semantic set of words.

1 | • "Often they were treated badly by other miners; some were the <u>victims of</u> violence." (par. 2)

• ". . . the Chinese often became the <u>victims of</u> discrimination." (par. 2)

• ". . . one of the largest groups of immigrants was the Irish; they were also <u>victims of</u> discrimination." (par. 3)

• "However, from around the middle of the nineteenth century, immigrants also began to <u>face</u> hostility from people already living in the United States." (par. 1)

• "Two immigrant groups who <u>faced</u> particular hardships were the Chinese and the Irish." (par. 1)

• "Most were escaping a terrible economic situation in Ireland, yet when they arrived in the United States, they also <u>faced</u> difficult conditions." (par. 3)

• "Each new group of immigrants that comes to the United States <u>faces</u> its own challenges." (par. 4)

• "Therefore, they are the immigrants who most frequently <u>face</u> anti-immigrant hostility and discrimination." (par. 4)

2 | **Answers**

victim of: violence, discrimination
face: hostility, hardships, difficult conditions, challenges, hostility and discrimination

3 | Students should glean that the collocating words usually describe something negative, dangerous, difficult, or challenging. If students need assistance, first have them sort the words into positive and negative.

Answers
victim of: *a $1,000 prize, a scholarship* do not collocate
face: *fun, great happiness* do not collocate

4 | Answers will vary.

Task 4 THINKING ABOUT THE TOPIC
This is another opportunity for students to display knowledge that others may not have. Encourage them to use some of the vocabulary used in this chapter.

UNIT 2 WRITING ASSIGNMENT A

Preparing to write (Student's Book pg. 72)

This writing task prompts learners to compare the experiences of various groups that have experienced difficulties in confronting the majority. There are obvious differences as well; in particular, Africans were the only group to experience the tragedy of slavery. Students will have a chance to explore those differences after they have finished the writing assignment.

1 | This is a short writing assignment, just one paragraph. Careful preparation will make the task much easier for students. If they fill in the chart well, they can pull all the information they need from it to complete their paragraph. If they can't fill in most of the boxes, go on to step 2.

Sample answers

	Hardships			
	Discrimination against this group at work	**Violence against this group**	**Cultural misunderstandings between this group and Americans**	**Other**
Native Americans		Trail of Tears	assimilationist policies	disease
Enslaved Africans	slavery	mistreatment, beatings of slaves		separation from family
Chinese	lower pay than Americans	violence in the workplace	misunderstanding of customs as strange and foreign	dangerous work
Irish	lower pay than Americans, refusal to hire them		Americans thought they were dirty, stupid, and lazy	dangerous work, long hours

2 | If students haven't been able to fill in most of the boxes, a discussion with classmates may help them complete the task.

3 | Check over your students' choices to make sure they have enough information to write a paragraph.

Now write

1 | Examples of opening phrases are provided in the Student's Book. It is fine if students choose to copy one of these.

2 | It is more important that students choose appropriate support for their claim than that they write in perfect English. Make sure they understand they must offer *two* hardships for each of the two groups they have chosen.

3 | Again, it is fine if they just wish to use the example provided. More adventurous or proficient students may prefer to try out one of their own.

4 | This step should mirror step 2.

5 | The order of writing may be the reverse of what you are accustomed to. However, for beginning writers, it is difficult to write an introductory sentence before they know what they are going to write about. Therefore, in this task, they write the supporting material before they write the introductory sentence that sums up the content of the paragraph.

6 | The paragraph may not be smooth, but it should contain all the necessary elements to make a claim and provide support for it.

Sample answer

In the nineteenth century, many ethnic and immigrant groups experienced difficulties in the United States. One problem that many immigrants faced was discrimination at work. Both the Irish and Chinese were forced to take the most difficult and low-paying jobs. In some cases, employers refused to hire Irish workers. These groups also often had bad experiences with people already living in the United States. The Chinese seemed very different to Americans who did not understand Chinese customs. The Irish also had different customs and traditions, and Americans believed they were lazy and stupid. This created a lot of hostility between Americans and the new immigrants.

After you write (Student's Book pg. 73)

1 | Again, students can benefit from looking at what others have written. Questions are very limited in scope and tailored for this particular assignment.

2 | At this point, students should limit their comments to the content.

3 | Having examined the similarities of immigrant groups, students should now be encouraged to address ways in which the experiences of these groups differed.

Chapter 4

Diversity in Today's United States

1 AMERICA'S INCREASINGLY DIVERSE FACE

Preparing to read (Student's Book pg. 74)

INCREASING YOUR READING SPEED

1 | Although much of the emphasis in this text is on reading comprehension, increasing speed is also an important goal for academic learners. Assist students by writing the start time on the board. You can ask them to write down their own finishing time or else you can write the time on the board as each minute passes.

2 | Have students calculate their reading rate.

3 | Reading quickly means little if there is no comprehension. Make sure students go back and check their answers after reading the text again.

Answers

1 more immigration outside of major cities; increase in immigration from Latin America and Asia

2 there have been changes in music, food, celebrities

3 *For*: immigrants contribute to prosperity, take jobs Americans don't want
Against: immigrants take jobs from Americans; they are a drain on public resources

Now read

Refer to page xi of this Teacher's Manual for suggestions about ways in which students can read the text.

After you read (Student's Book pg. 77)

Task 1 SCANNING

Review the importance and meaning of scanning for specific information.

Answers

1 12 percent, lower **2** Mexico **3** 32 million **4** 7 **5** buying homes, starting businesses, paying taxes

Task 2 LANGUAGE FOCUS: REDUCED ADJECTIVE CLAUSES

Students may be familiar with these clauses as *relative clauses*. *Adjective clause* is a somewhat more transparent term, so we use it here. This is not an exhaustive lesson on adjective clauses or on participial phrases. The goal is for learners to recognize one new form of modification of noun phrases that is common in academic writing. It is not expected that they will be able to produce adjective clauses. Resist the urge to explain everything here.

1 | Do the example for the class to make sure everyone understands.

   Answers

   2 Approximately 12 percent of **the people** <u>living in the United States</u> were born in another country. (who live in the United States)

   3 There are **82 international team members** <u>playing for the NBA</u>. (who play for the NBA)

   4 **Many people** <u>working in high technology companies</u> were born in other countries. (who work in high technology companies)

   5 **Immigrants** <u>hoping for economic opportunity</u> began arriving in the American colonies in the seventeenth century. (who hoped for economic opportunity)

2 | **Sample answers**

   1 Students <u>taking important exams</u> should try to sleep well the night before.

   2 People <u>learning a second language</u> should watch television programs in the second language.

   3 Tourists <u>visiting New York</u> should go to the Metropolitan Museum of Art.

   4 People <u>earning more than 1 million dollars a year</u> should give some of their money to the poor.

Task 3 THINKING ABOUT THE TOPIC

Many Americans are familiar with these metaphors from their elementary school days, but they will be novel for some students. You may need to explain the meaning of a patchwork quilt and how the pieces come from diverse sources.

Sample answers

1 Response should include some discussion that the salad and quilt metaphors allow groups to maintain individual characteristics at the same time as they become American, in contrast to the melting pot.

2 Answers will vary, but students should give reasons for their choices.

3 Answers will vary, but students should give reasons for their choices.

2 LATINOS: THE COUNTRY'S LARGEST MINORITY GROUP

Preparing to read (Student's Book pg. 79)

EXAMINING GRAPHIC MATERIAL

1 | **Answers**
Southwest/West: proximity to Mexico and Central America

2 | Answers should include the following information: It shows the projected increase in the Hispanic population as well as a projected increase in the percentage of the population of the United States that will be Hispanic.

Now read

Refer to page xi of this Teacher's Manual for suggestions about ways in which students can read the text. Refer students who wish to identify the states to the map on page xxi of the Student's Book.

After you read (Student's Book pg. 82)

Task 1 TEST TAKING: ANSWERING TRUE/FALSE QUESTIONS

1,2 | This is the next task in the series on test taking. True/false test questions are common in academic settings and there are strategies learners can use to answer them. Students may have experience with such test items but they may not have considered strategies for success.

Answers

T 1 map   T 3 par. 2   T 5 par. 2   F 7 par. 1

F 2 map   F 4 par. 1   T 6 Fig. 4.1   T 8 par. 3

Task 2 NOTE TAKING: USING AN OUTLINE

1 | This is a task to support comprehension, but the primary goal here is note taking. Outlining is a good way for students to review the material in a text and also to prepare for tests and writing assignments. Make sure students close their books while they are completing the outline so they are not tempted to copy the text. Explain to students that complete sentences are not necessary in an outline and that abbreviations and symbols are OK to use.

Sample answers

    I. There has been a big increase in the Latino population in the United States since 1990. (par. 1 main idea)

        A. Latinos have become the largest minority. (par. 1 evidence)

        B. Latino pop. has increased by 58%, 7 times the growth rate for the rest of pop. (par. 1 evidence)

        C. % has grown from 18 to 42. (par. 1 evidence)

        D. Some areas have had growth up to 300%. (par. 1 evidence)

    II. This growth has caused changes in everyday life. (par. 2 main idea)

        A. Changes in popular culture (par. 2 evidence)

        B. Changes in the economy (par. 2 evidence)

        C. Increase in political influence (par. 2 evidence)

   III. The Spanish language has become more important. (par. 3 main idea)

        A. Many businesses want Spanish-speaking employees. (par. 3 evidence)

        B. Many Americans study Spanish. (par. 3 evidence)

        C. Americans use Spanish expressions. (par. 3 evidence)

2 | Give students time to compare answers with a partner.

Task 3 LANGUAGE FOCUS: THE *-ING* FORM OF THE VERB AS AN ADJECTIVE

1 | Students may not be familiar with the participle as an adjective. This only works with specific verbs, but it is not crucial that you explain this. The goal here is that they should recognize the *-ing* form as a form of modification.

Answers

1 At least 28 cities across the country have (growing) Latino populations.

2 The (increasing) number of Latinos is causing cultural, economic, and political change.

3 Many businesses are looking for (Spanish-speaking) employees.

2 | This is a modest step in the direction of production. Free and spontaneous production of these forms is not expected at this point.

Answers

2 the rising popularity of Mexican food

3 the increasing ethnic diversity in the United States

4 the growing economic influence of the Latino community

3 THE UNDOCUMENTED: ILLEGAL IMMIGRANTS

Preparing to read (Student's Book pg. 84)

SKIMMING: FIRST SENTENCES, GRAPHIC MATERIALS, AND ART

1,2 | Students' notes will vary, but they should include these facts: the increase in the number of undocumented residents; the reasons for illegal immigration; and the arguments for and against it. In addition, students should include the idea that illegal immigration poses dangers for those who try it.

3 | Give students time to compare notes with a partner.

BUILDING BACKGROUND KNOWLEDGE OF THE TOPIC

1 | Students should grasp the idea that coyotes are both intelligent and dangerous. They may guess that coyotes are part of the illegal immigration business.

2 | *smuggling*: taking things to or from a place secretly and illegally. Students should understand that *human smuggling* means taking *people* to or from a place secretly and illegally.

Now read

Refer to page xi of this Teacher's Manual for suggestions about ways in which students can read the text. Give students time to review their notes.

After you read (Student's Book pg. 87)

Task 1 READING LITERATURE ABOUT A TOPIC

This excerpt includes the opening lines from a well-known nonfiction account of the experiences and deaths of several would-be illegal immigrants, abandoned in the desert by their coyote. You may want to provide your students with more context for this excerpt; in particular, the dangers of crossing the desert.

Sample answers

1 illegal immigrants

2 mountain pass, lost, barefoot

3 sets the context, describes the dangers

4 the personal, physical experience is clearer in the excerpt

Task 2 THINKING ABOUT THE TOPIC

This is an opportunity for students to express their views and to bring any specific knowledge they have about similar situations in other settings.

Task 3 LANGUAGE FOCUS: WRITING ABOUT HISTORICAL TRENDS

The use of the present perfect is far more complex than what is presented here. This is simply an effort to get learners to recognize some basic differences between the simple past and the present perfect.

1 | Answers

	Tense	Time period	Is the time period over?
1a. Since September 11, 2001, the nation has increased security at its borders . . .	PP	Sept. 11, 2001–present	No
1b. . . . and crossing illegally has become even more difficult and dangerous.	PP	Sept. 11, 2001–present	No
2. Business for coyotes has grown dramatically in recent years.	PP	recently	No
3. In 2003, these smugglers moved about 1 million illegal immigrants from nearly 100 countries across the border.	P	2003	Yes
4. The human-smuggling industry earned $9.5 billion that year [2003], according to immigration officials.	P	2003	Yes
5. Many illegal immigrants have died trying to cross into the United States...	PP	not stated	No
6. More than 2,500 people died between 1997 and 2004 in attempts to enter the United States illegally.	P	1997–2004	Yes

2 | Make sure that students understand that their responses may entail some minor calculations.

Sample answers

These answers are for 2007 (2008 figures are in parentheses).

1 Since 2003, about 2 million (about 2.5 million) illegal immigrants have entered the United States.

2 Since 2000, about 1.75 million (more than 2 million) Mexicans have entered the United States illegally.

3 Since the 1990 census, the percentage of illegal immigrants that live in California has dropped from 50 percent to 33 percent.

4 LINGUISTIC DIVERSITY OR ENGLISH ONLY?

Preparing to read (Student's Book pg. 89)

THINKING ABOUT THE TOPIC BEFORE YOU READ

Students may have very little idea about language policy and linguistic diversity in the United States. They should draw on the knowledge they have gained from the text thus far. This activity could be done in pairs so students can pool their knowledge.

1 | **Answers**

F 1   T 2   T 3   T 4   F 5   F 6   T 7   F 8

2 | This is another opportunity for open-ended discussion and for students to offer their individual knowledge and experiences. You may want to have them look at the photos that accompany the text and ask where they think these scenes are located. Answer to 1: 82 percent

Now read

Refer to page xi of this Teacher's Manual for suggestions about ways in which students can read the text. After students have finished, be sure they check their answers.

➡ Remind students to review and update their vocabulary notebooks.

After you read (Student's Book pg. 92)

Task 1 THINKING CRITICALLY ABOUT THE TOPIC

This discussion could just as easily take place with the whole class. It brings together many of the issues that have been raised throughout this unit, this time regarding language. Be sure that students support their claims with reasons, not just single word responses or yes/no. If there are divergent views in the class, this can generate useful and interesting discussion.

Task 2 LANGUAGE FOCUS: VERBS TO USE INSTEAD OF *SAY* AND *THINK*

One of the marks of high proficiency in academic language is lexical variety and the use of lower frequency words instead of high-coverage, high-frequency words. Two of the most commonly overused words are *say* and *think*.

1 | **Answers**
The following sentences in the text contain synonyms for *say* and *think*.

... They <u>contend</u> that English is an important factor in national identity. They also <u>maintain</u> that the use of other languages will cause division among different ethnic communities. ... However, ... they <u>argue</u> that government services in any language other than English should not be permitted. ... (par. 3)

Supporters of linguistic diversity <u>believe</u> English-only laws are based on prejudice against ethnic minorities. They <u>claim</u> that these laws force immigrants to give up their own cultural identity to become American. They <u>argue</u> that multilingual services help new immigrants adjust to life in the United States. . . . Just as importantly, they <u>maintain</u> that the language skills of immigrants are a great national resource. . . . Those who support linguistic diversity <u>argue</u> that this resource should not be lost. . . . The *New York Times* quotes one scholar who <u>contends</u> that the United States is a "language graveyard." (par. 4)

2 | This task gives students a chance to use new vocabulary in context and to recycle previous content. Although the objective is for them to use the new vocabulary, they may need some assistance in formulating the clauses following the *say* verbs.

Sample answers

a Some Americans <u>argue</u> that <u>we cannot stop illegal immigration</u>. They <u>maintain</u> that illegal immigrants <u>will continue to come in spite of efforts to stop them</u>. They also <u>contend</u> that <u>immigrant labor is important for the economy</u>.

b Some Americans <u>believe</u> that <u>it is both possible and necessary to limit illegal immigration into the United States</u>. These opponents of illegal immigration <u>maintain</u> that undocumented workers <u>take jobs from Americans</u>. They also <u>argue</u> that <u>illegal immigrants are expensive because they need services like health care and education</u>.

3 | Compare answers as a class.

UNIT 2 WRITING ASSIGNMENT B

Preparing to write (Student's Book pg. 93)

1 | *Ambivalence* is the central concept in this assignment so it is important that students understand it. Here is one definition of *ambivalent* from the *Cambridge Advanced Learner's Dictionary* at www.dictionary.cambridge.org: "having two opposing feelings at the same time." Students should make reference to the fact that through history there have been both positive and negative attitudes toward immigration and diversity.

2 | There are many possible ways to fill out these columns. Be sure students have strong enough examples to support the writing assignment.

Sample answer

Positive attitudes/action	Negative attitudes/action
Pride in ethnic heritage	Anti-immigration opinions
Acceptance of aspects of different cultures such as music and food	Quotas to limit immigration
	English-only laws
Services for non-English speakers	Violence toward/fear of immigrants

Now write

By now students should have a good idea about how to draw on evidence to support their claims, but they still may need help in framing the claim. It may be easier to write the supporting sentences first and write the introductory sentence afterward. Similarly, this assignment is structured to write the body paragraphs before the paragraph that introduces them. Students may find this strange, but, in fact, it makes sense. Unless you are an experienced writer, it is difficult to figure out how to introduce material that you have not yet written.

1 | **Sample answer**

Many Americans feel positive about their multicultural country. Americans and their families have come from many different parts of the world, and they are proud of that heritage. They welcome customs from other parts of the world, such as music, art, and food. They continue to welcome new immigrants by providing services that will help them adjust to life in their new country.

2 | **Sample answer**

However, Americans have also had negative attitudes toward ethnic diversity. Many Americans oppose the continuing high rate of immigration and would like to have more secure borders. Some Americans are angry about immigration because they think immigrants are an economic burden. Some also think immigrants are changing the country too much, especially the language. They want all immigrants to learn English.

3 | This step may be more difficult. Make sure students understand that this short paragraph has to orient the reader to both of the paragraphs they have written. It is important that students know that conveying the concept of ambivalence is the key to doing this effectively.

Sample answer

Americans have often been ambivalent about the multicultural character of their nation. American history shows changing attitudes toward immigration. Today, that feeling of ambivalence continues. Some Americans feel positive about the county's ethnic heritage and diversity. Other Americans are more negative about the topic.

4 | This step and schematic representation may seem somewhat mechanical, but it is useful to students to have patterns and this kind of concrete support at this early stage of writing.

After you write (Student's Book pg. 94)

1 | As always, the best peer-feedback questions ask writers to do something specific. Students should avoid vague but evaluative language such as *good* and *like*. You may wish to ask peer editors to point to specific evidence in the writing to answer questions 3 and 4.

2 | At this point, peers can offer more personal opinions if you have time and feel it would be useful to the writers.

The Struggle for Equality

Unit title page (Student's Book pg. 95)

Make sure that students understand the meaning of the unit title. Ask them about their understanding of the word *struggle* and explain how it is related to, but different from, *fight*.

Give students time to read the unit summary paragraph and check to be sure they understand the areas the unit will cover.

Previewing the unit (Student's Book pg. 96)

Chapter 5: The Struggle Begins

Even for older Americans, signs like the one in the photograph come as a surprise. Americans and non-Americans alike tend to think of this period as remote history. Answers will vary, but encourage students to see that the boy peering through the door in the photograph personalizes the pain and humiliation of segregation.

Chapter 6: The Struggle Continues

1 | This activity functions in one of two ways: If the country in focus is the United States, it can be a myth buster. If other countries are in focus, it gives learners a chance to show their individual expertise and knowledge.

2 | This can also be done as a whole-class activity.

The Struggle Begins

1 ALL MEN ARE CREATED EQUAL

Preparing to read (Student's Book pg. 98)

THINKING ABOUT THE TOPIC BEFORE YOU READ

This activity builds on the "Previewing the unit" task in its focus on equality. Many people think that the concept is both self-evident and static. This discussion should help students understand that it is neither.

BUILDING BACKGROUND KNOWLEDGE OF THE TOPIC

1 | The concept of natural rights may be difficult for students who have never heard of or thought about it. It may be helpful to elicit some examples from them and, if they are unable to produce any, to suggest some of your own. These run along the lines of life, liberty, the pursuit of happiness, and the rights enumerated in the Declaration of Independence. These will be specifically discussed in the text.

2 | **Sample answers**

  1 Encourage students to include the idea that equality comes with being a human being; it is not anything that someone else bestows upon you. This idea, according to Jefferson, should be the foundation of government. Some students may offer the idea that equality is God-given. In fact, this is consistent with the founders' views.

  2 A complete response might include the thoughts that Jefferson's ideas were in contrast with earlier views that suggested even basic rights are unevenly distributed. In addition, these same rights may be conferred on one person by another and, by the same logic, taken away. This concept was at the foundation of many European governments at that time.

Now read

Refer to page xi of this Teacher's Manual for suggestions about ways in which students can read the text.

After you read (Student's Book pg. 101)

Task 1 READING FOR MAIN IDEAS

This task follows up on the questions from the "Preparing to read" tasks now that students have more information.

1 | Answers will vary but should include the following:
   1 They thought it meant that God makes everyone equal at birth, but their view of "everyone" was different from ours today.

   2 Before this time, most people accepted inequality as natural.

   3 It included African Americans.

   4 No, unequal treatment continued for many Americans. Students may point out particular examples, such as African Americans and women.

2 | You may prefer to discuss this with the whole class.

Task 2 BUILDING VOCABULARY: SUFFIXES THAT CHANGE VERBS AND ADJECTIVES INTO NOUNS

This idea is probably familiar to most students, so this task will serve as a review.

1 | **Answers**
   1 "The most famous lines of the <u>Declaration</u> of Independence . . ."

   2 "They brought together ideas from many different sources . . . that had democratic systems of <u>government</u>."

   3 "The <u>disagreements</u> between the North and the South . . ."

   4 "The Fourteenth <u>Amendment</u> to the Constitution was passed . . ."

   5 "It guarantees equal <u>protection</u> of the law to everyone . . ."

2 | **Answers**
   1 "But what did the term *equality* really mean when the nation began?"

   2 "The most famous lines in the Declaration of <u>Independence</u> . . ."

3 | **Answers**
   1 diverse   **2** contribution   **3** define   **4** equal

4 | This step recycles vocabulary and content from previous chapters and requires students to apply what they have learned in the first three steps. They may have to look back over earlier texts.

Answers

1 settled   **5** popularity

2 hostility   **6** persecution

3 violence   **7** punish

4 significant

5 Answers will vary. Some of the clues are based on how well the meaning fits, or collocates, with one of the choices (e.g., *violence against*); others are primarily syntactic (e.g., *to* suggests that a verb will follow).

2 THE LEGACY OF THE CIVIL WAR

Preparing to read (Student's Book pg. 103)

BUILDING VOCABULARY: PREVIEWING KEY TERMS

1 Knowing the meaning of these key words is crucial to understanding the text. These definitions are from the *Cambridge Advanced Learner's Dictionary* at www.dictionary.cambridge.org.
- *discriminate*: to treat a person or particular group of people differently, especially in a worse way from the way in which you treat other people, because of their skin color, religion, gender, etc.
- *disenfranchise*: to take away power or opportunities, especially the right to vote, from a person or group of people
- *segregate*: to keep one group of people apart from another and treat them differently, especially because of race or gender
- *separate*: to force people to move apart or to different places; to move apart

2 **Answers**

1 discrimination, segregation

2 It is important for students to understand this distinction. *Separation* simply means keeping people or groups apart. *Segregation* means separation for the purpose of treating people differently.

3 Answers will vary, but may include instances in education or employment.

4 Students may recall that in the past, both women and Native Americans were prevented from voting.

3 The *Cambridge Advanced Learner's Dictionary* offers the following definition of *legacy*: something that is a part of your history or which stays from an earlier time. Any similar idea will suffice.

Now read

Refer to page xi of this Teacher's Manual for suggestions about ways in which students can read the text.

After you read (Student's Book pg. 106)

Task 1 READING TO FIND SUPPORT FOR MAIN IDEAS

1 | This task gives students an opportunity to practice a skill that was introduced in Chapter 3. It is important for students to see that these skills are useful beyond the original task. Try to have students practice some form of note taking for each text.

Answers

1 "It is estimated that there were almost 5,000 lynchings between 1882 and 1968." (par. 6)

2 "The South also had a more unequal social structure, that is, a small upper class and a large class of people on the bottom – poor farmers and slaves. The Southern economy depended heavily on slave labor." (par. 1)

3 "These schools were usually not very good because they did not receive as much money from the government as white schools did." (par. 5)

4 "There were not very many businesses that served African Americans." (boxed text)

5 "However, the civil and political rights of African Americans were gradually taken away because states in the South began to pass laws that limited these rights." (par. 2)

Task 2 BUILDING VOCABULARY: KEY TERMS

1 | Make sure students close their books. Encourage them to take notes on what their partners say. Doing so may help them with the second step of this task.

2 | It is fine for students to repeat the noun in the definition; that is, Jim Crow *laws* were *laws* . . .

Sample answers

1 **Jim Crow laws** were laws that maintained segregation and discrimination against blacks.

2 **Literacy tests** were tests that required people to show they could read before they were allowed to vote.

3 A **voting tax** was a tax that people were required to pay in order to vote.

4 **Grandfather laws** were laws that permitted those people with a grandparent who had voted to avoid other voting laws.

5 A **lynching** is a murder by a mob of people who decide a person is guilty of a crime or bad behavior.

3 | If students are having difficulty making this generalization, you may want to have a brief class discussion so that they can collaborate on the solution.

Sample answer

These were all steps that Southern states took to make it difficult or impossible for African Americans to vote.

3 THE BATTLE FOR CIVIL RIGHTS

Preparing to read (Student's Book pg. 107)

READING LITERATURE ABOUT A TOPIC

1 | The sentiment of this evocative poem should be accessible to students of all levels of proficiency. If you would like to give your students more information about this poet, the Annenberg Voices and Visions Web site, which is cited in the footnote, has a great deal of background information on Hughes in addition to a video clip of a reading of the poem. Do encourage students to listen to the reading if they have access to the Internet.

2 | Responses will vary to all of these questions, but students should understand that Hughes was referring to the experience of black Americans, as well as to the more general condition of dreams that are put off for too long.

Now read

Refer to page xi of this Teacher's Manual for suggestions about ways in which students can read the text.

After you read (Student's Book pg. 110)

Task 1 NOTE TAKING: HIGHLIGHTING

This task gives more specific instruction on effective highlighting. In addition, the task follows the process further, so students can see the utility of this method. Highlighted material may differ from student to student but should include school desegregation, the various forms of the civil rights movement, and its culmination in acts of Congress.

Task 2 TEST TAKING: UNDERSTANDING THE LANGUAGE OF TEST QUESTIONS

1 | Deconstructing the language of test questions is the first step in answering them. It is not always obvious what a question is asking.

2 | Answers will vary.

Task 3 TEST TAKING: ANSWERING TEST QUESTIONS

1 Although this is laid out in step 2 of this activity, you might ask students what they notice about the language of these sentences and how they relate to the original test questions.

2 **Sample answers**

1 The lawyers defending segregation in the *Brown versus Board of Education of Topeka* case offered two main arguments.

2 The strategies of the civil rights movement consisted of court battles and street protests.

3 The economies of the northern and southern states before the U.S. Civil War were very different.

3 Answers will vary.

4 Writing out the entire answer may be too challenging, but students should be able to discuss more informally what the rest of their responses would include.

Task 4 THINKING CRITICALLY ABOUT THE TOPIC

Students' answers will vary, but answers should convey the idea that King is more hopeful that his dream will be fulfilled, compared to Hughes, who is more focused on what happens when dreams are not fulfilled. For both of them, the dream includes equal treatment and respect for people of color, which is the focus of much of this chapter.

4 THE WOMEN'S MOVEMENT

Preparing to read (Student's Book pg. 112)

THINKING ABOUT THE TOPIC BEFORE YOU READ

1 Answers will vary, but should include the idea that the overall situation for women has improved and that they receive more equal treatment than they did 50 years ago. Draw students' attention to the caption beneath the picture on page 113. Ask them if the quote is familiar.

2 **Sample answers**

1 A fish does not need a bicycle. → Women don't need men.

2 She does not like them perhaps because they restrict the wearer's movement and they are uncomfortable. Their main purpose is to make legs look longer and more attractive.

Now read

Refer to page xi of this Teacher's Manual for suggestions about ways in which students can read the text.

➡ Remind students to review and update their vocabulary notebooks.

After you read (Student's Book pg. 115)

Task 1 SCANNING

Remind students what scanning means and that they should not read every word of the text.

Sample answers

	1960	**Today**
Average age of marriage for women	20	25
Average number of children for women	3–4	"fewer"
Percentage of working people who are women	a minority – text does not specify	more than 50 percent
Percentage of college students who are women	a minority – text does not specify	slightly more than 50 percent
Percentage of medical students who are women	10 percent	about 50 percent

Task 2 LANGUAGE FOCUS: TIME CONNECTORS

Students are often confused because the same words (e.g., *before, after*) can have different syntactic functions. Yet, *during* and *while* are not interchangeable in terms of syntactic function. This is difficult for students to discover on their own.

1 | Identifying these features is the first step.

Sample answers
- "*After* the war, most women were asked to leave their jobs and let the men return to work." (preposition, par. 2)
- "*During* the war (1939–1945), thousands of women joined the workforce because they were needed in the factories *while* the men were away at war." (subordinator, par. 2)

2 | **Answers**
   1 After the Civil War / After the Civil War ended
   2 During
   3 Before World War II / Before the war began

3 | Answers will vary.

Task 3 EXAMINING GRAPHIC MATERIAL

1 | Three-dimensional graphs are difficult to interpret. The fact that "men of the same ethnicity" is the baseline for comparison compounds the difficulty of this graph. You may need to get students started by beginning this task together as a class.

2 | **Sample answers**

   1 Compared to other ethnic groups, the difference between white women's and white men's pay is the greatest.

   2 As a group, women earn between 60 percent and 90 percent of what men of the same ethnicity earn.

   3 In general, women made little progress toward wage equality with men between 1998 and 2000.

UNIT 3 WRITING ASSIGNMENT A

Preparing to write (Student's Book pg. 117)

Students will be using the material from Chapter 5 to write a three-paragraph paper. They should consult the notes they have made throughout the chapter as they consider their position regarding the relationship of voting and equality.

1 | Encourage students to take more notes as they discuss the questions in preparation for writing. Items 1, 2, and 3 are designed to elicit the following discussions:
   • Why is voting so important? Does it really confer an advantage?
   • Reconsider the importance/advantage of voting in light of what students have learned about African Americans.
   • Reconsider the importance/advantage of voting in light of what students have learned about the women's movement.

2 | Any of these points of view can be argued using the evidence offered in Chapter 5. The main goal is for students to choose the appropriate evidence to support their point of view. The third point of view, although probably the easiest to argue based on the facts, may present the most difficulty in terms of the structure of the paper. Students who choose that one may need a little extra guidance.

Now write

The second and third paragraphs correspond to the second and third discussions in step 1 of "Preparing to write." For the first two paragraphs, the Student's Book offers possible ways to begin the topic sentences. Encourage stronger students to write their own, but allow students who struggle with writing to use the frames provided.

Sample paper

In the United States, winning the right to vote was an important step in the struggle for equality for African Americans and women. Voting has allowed them to participate more in American society. Both groups fought for this right so they could have a voice in government and protect their own rights. The history of African Americans and women are good examples of the importance of the right to vote.

African Americans have achieved equality in many areas since they won the right to vote, but these achievements did not occur right away. Although amendments to the Constitution gave African Americans the right to vote, many states passed laws that made voting almost impossible. Jim Crow laws also restricted their access to education and public facilities. Starting in the 1960s, court decisions ended segregation in schools and in public places. Now blacks and whites go to the same schools and use the same public spaces. Most important, blacks now have a voice in their government and in their own future. They can elect leaders who will help them.

The right to vote has also increased equality for women, but, as with African Americans, progress has not always been fast. Women started voting in 1920, but many of them still did not get a good education. Many more women are getting a good education today. There has also been progress in employment. The law says that women should receive the same pay as men if they have the same job. Their pay has increased a lot. However, women still earn less than men for the same work.

After you write (Student's Book pg. 118)

1 | This is an important step and a habit students should cultivate. Many student writers hand in their assignment directly after writing. Make sure they understand the importance of rereading their work – not just for grammar problems, but for content as well – before handing it in. You may also want to discuss the advantage of putting a paper away for a while and returning to it later. This gives students time to reflect as well as provides the distance that is often helpful in the editing process.

2 | Starting with this assignment, students are asked to focus on surface-level features as well as the content and structure of their writing. However, editing can be an overwhelming task, so this assignment requires them to address just one item. If they are unsure, then you should choose one for them. Make sure it is a problem that they *can* correct on their own. Good choices usually include tense shifting and subject-verb agreement. Students should begin making a list of these choices for review in subsequent assignments.

3, 4 | Although these steps are designed as part of the peer editing process, a concurrent goal is to get students to edit their own papers. If their partner cannot find the claim and the evidence, it is probably not clear. Suggest that in future assignments, students try this with their own writing before beginning peer review.

Chapter

The Struggle Continues

1 WHAT DOES EQUALITY MEAN TODAY?

Preparing to read (Student's Book pg. 119)

BUILDING VOCABULARY: PREVIEWING KEY TERMS

1 | You may want to start the activity as a whole class and point out words in context that can help students. For example, in the first item, the phrase "against minority students" suggests the meaning of *biased*.

2 | **Answers**

   _d_ **1**

   _e_ **2**

   _b_ **3**

   _c_ **4**

   _a_ **5**

3 | Students should include in their discussion that equality would mean that all people have *access* to *resources*. The question of *merit* is somewhat more contentious: Should it be the basis of equal treatment? This is something that is addressed at length in this chapter.

Now read

Refer to page xi of this Teacher's Manual for suggestions about ways in which students can read the text.

After you read (Student's Book pg. 122)

Task 1 SUMMARIZING

It is important to note that this is just an introduction to summarizing, which is a skill that takes a very long time to master. It is not expected that students will be able to summarize quickly or even well after this task. The task provides a considerable amount of linguistic support, and it will be some time before students will be able to do this independently.

1 | Students may be tempted to think that (c) is best, but that is not the intention of the text. The text simply describes three positions. The answer is (b).

2 | This step will be difficult for students, and it is not expected that their production will be error-free.

Sample answers

1 One interpretation of equality is there are no differences among people.

2 A second definition is that everyone should have equal access and opportunity.

3 A third view is that there should be equal outcomes with equal opportunity.

3 | **Sample answer**

The text "What Does Equality Mean Today?" presents three different interpretations of the word *equality*. One interpretation of equality is there are no differences among people. A second definition is that everyone should have equal access and opportunity. A third view is that there should be equal outcomes with equal opportunity.

Task 2 LANGUAGE FOCUS: *SHOULD*

Students often overuse the modal *must* where *should* is more appropriate, especially in academic writing. This task focuses their attention on the use of *should* for offering recommendations.

1 | **Answers**

- "Does it mean that Americans <u>should</u> all have an equal opportunity to compete for resources, such as jobs, housing, and education?" (par. 1)
- "Or does it mean that all Americans <u>should</u> end up equal – in other words, that resources <u>should</u> be spread equally across all people in the country, regardless of who they are?" (par. 1)
- ". . . everyone <u>should</u> have an equal opportunity to succeed and equal access to resources." (par. 3)
- "<u>Should</u> the government try to ensure that there are not only equal opportunities but equal results, too?" (par. 5)
- "If so, how <u>should</u> they do this?" (par. 5)
- "<u>Should</u> the city ignore the program and simply guarantee a certain number of positions in the police department to women?" (par. 6)

2 | **Sample answers**

Businesses should try to hire minority and women employees.
The government should make more money available for minority education programs.

3 | **Sample answers**
Minorities should not be asked to meet different standards.
Businesses should not be forced to hire people just because they are minorities.

Task 3 BUILDING VOCABULARY: SYNONYMS

Lexical variety is an important feature of academic writing. It is a good idea to get students to build up their knowledge of different ways of saying the same thing. Make sure they are using their vocabulary notebooks.

1 | **Answers**

  1 "Will that <u>ensure</u> equality? History suggests that equal opportunity does not always (guarantee) equal outcomes." (par. 4)

  2 ". . . this will hurt the African-American children's <u>chances</u> to succeed because there is unequal access to resources and (opportunities)." (par. 3)

  3 ". . . resources should be <u>spread</u> equally across all people in the country, regardless of who they are?" (par. 1) "This is a problem the government can try to correct by (distributing) resources more fairly." (par. 4)

  4 "History suggests that equal opportunity does not always guarantee equal <u>outcomes</u>." (par. 4) "Should the government try to ensure that there are not only equal opportunities but equal (results), too?" (par. 5)

  5 ". . . providing better schools has not necessarily <u>led to</u> equal success for African Americans." (par. 4) "Equal opportunity has not (resulted in) equal outcomes . . ." (par. 6)

  6 "The second <u>view</u> says that although we are all different, none of those differences matters . . ." (par. 3) "We therefore need to consider a third (perspective) on equality." (par. 4)

2 | Answers will vary.

Task 4 LANGUAGE FOCUS: MARKERS OF DEPENDENCY

The differences among these markers are sometimes subtle and therefore difficult to grasp based on input alone. In fact, *depending on* and *based on* are sometimes interchangeable.

1 | **Answers**

  1 Everyone should have access to a good education <u>regardless of</u> race.

  2 The economic success of minority groups varies <u>depending on</u> the part of the country in which they live. (*based on* would also be acceptable)

  3 Unfortunately, some employers make hiring decisions <u>based on</u> the ethnicity of the applicant.

2 | **Sample answers**

  1 His decision was based on <u>many factors</u>.

  2 Regardless of your opinion, <u>you should consider the opinions of other people</u>.

  3 Depending on the weather, <u>we may take a picnic lunch</u>.

2 AFFIRMATIVE ACTION

Preparing to read (Student's Book pg. 124)

BRAINSTORMING

Students may have already started thinking about this in Task 2 of the previous section. They will be drawing on these ideas throughout this chapter, so this task is designed to get them started.

BRAINSTORMING: ORGANIZING YOUR IDEAS

Brainstorming is frequently used as a prewriting strategy. However, it is only useful insofar as students are able to draw on the ideas they generate. It is important to guide students in the next step of organizing the ideas that are the product of the brainstorming session.

Now read

Refer to page xi of this Teacher's Manual for suggestions about ways in which students can read the text.

After you read (Student's Book pg. 127)

Task 1 UNDERSTANDING THE FUNCTION OF DIFFERENT PARTS OF THE TEXT

This task pushes students' comprehension beyond looking for specific pieces of information to understanding why each section is included in the text. This is useful not only as part of reading comprehension training but also in preparation for writing. If students have difficulty finishing this step on their own, encourage them to collaborate with a classmate.

1 | **Answers**

1 Explains the argument in favor of affirmative action _par. 7_

2 Gives a definition of affirmative action _par. 3_

3 Describes an example of affirmative action _par. 1_

4 Expands the definition of affirmative action _par. 4_

5 Describes an example of a successful fight against affirmative action _BT_

6 Explains the goals of affirmative action _par. 5_

7 Explains an argument against affirmative action _par. 8_

8 Discusses the difficulty of making affirmative action decisions _par. 2_

9 Give reasons for the controversy about affirmative action _par. 9_

10 Describes the success of affirmative action programs _par. 6_

2 You may need to review the arguments from the first text in this chapter to help students answer the first question. The answers to the other four questions can be retrieved fairly easily from the current text.

Sample answers

1 Everyone should end up equal. / There should be equal outcomes.

2 It helps even out unequal backgrounds and historical experience.

3 It constitutes special treatment of certain groups at the expense of others and is therefore unequal treatment.

4 Programs are controversial because of the conflict between self-reliance/ individual merit and equal opportunity.

5 Bakke believed he was a victim of discrimination because he was *not* a minority.

Task 2 APPLYING WHAT YOU HAVE READ

As the title suggests, this task pushes learners beyond comprehension and retrieval and asks them to apply the ideas from the text to new material. The quote from Justice Blackmun is from the *Bakke* ruling. Thernstrom is a Harvard professor known for his views opposing affirmative action, similar to those of Justice Clarence Thomas. This is a difficult task; it may be necessary to have a teacher-led discussion.

Sample answers

1 Racism makes special treatment necessary in order to guarantee equal results.

2 Individuals should not be treated specially just because they can be identified by a group: African Americans, women, and so on.

3 They represent the two opposing points of view.

4 Blackmun – for; Thernstrom – against

Task 3 DEBATING THE TOPIC

1 Debates do not work with every class or with every topic. Depending on how your students have responded to this material, you will need to decide if this is an appropriate task for your class. If they have found the material compelling, by now, each student should have developed clear views on the topic. Perhaps you will even have some students on each side of the issue.

2 Decide how you want to run your debate. One common method is to have each side do a three-to-five-minute presentation, then give each side a chance to rebut the other's position. In order to do this, students must (1) prepare their speeches and (2) anticipate the arguments of the other side. Make sure they understand that their speeches should contain a claim (the language in step 3 will be useful for this) and support for that claim, probably in the form of examples. Students should have written notes.

3 | Students should work from notes, but they should not read their statements. If they are ambitious and have adequate resources, they may want to complement their presentations with slides or other graphics. If there are other instructors available, students can debate in a more public way, with another teacher judging the winner. Alternatively, if only a part of the class is debating, the rest of the class can act as judges. If you decide to use the class as judges, it is important that the listeners know what to look for and on what basis they should select a winner. You might want to consider a listener's sheet, on which the judges can rate various features of the debate.

3 TRYING NOT TO BE SPECIAL: AMERICANS WITH DISABILITIES

Preparing to read (Student's Book pg. 129)

THINKING ABOUT THE TOPIC BEFORE YOU READ

Depending on students' backgrounds, they may already be familiar with many of the symbols and ways of accommodating the disabled. If students don't know the term *disabled*, they may know the Christopher Reeve story, so you can turn to the end of the text if you think this will help them understand. Accommodation for the disabled varies considerably in different parts of the world, so this can make for a lively discussion. Be sure students understand and can discuss the meaning of the terms *disabled* and *accommodation*.

Now read

Refer to page xi of this Teacher's Manual for suggestions about ways in which students can read the text.

After you read (Student's Book pg. 132)

Task 1 APPLYING WHAT YOU HAVE READ

If students have difficulty with this, point to key words, such as *building* (item 2) and *subway* (item 5), which are important clues.

Answers

PF **1**

PF **2**

TC **3**

G **4**

TP **5**

E **6**

Task 2 LANGUAGE FOCUS: INTRODUCING EXAMPLES WITH *FOR EXAMPLE* AND *SUCH AS*

These are common sources of confusion for beginning writers, in part because it is difficult to glean the rules from input alone. If students make such mistakes in their writing, encourage them to return to this task for reference.

1 | **Answers**

   ✓ 1

   ✓ 2

   ✗ 3

   ✓ 4

   ✗ 5

   ✗ 6

2 | Answers will vary.

Task 3 THINKING CRITICALLY ABOUT THE TOPIC

1 | You might take the opportunity to discuss euphemisms and language change, and how we no longer use some of the terms that were common in earlier times. You could recall the use of the word *Negro* in an earlier chapter. This Bruegel painting and the photograph of disabled athletes are dramatic examples of changing attitudes toward disability.

2 | These discussion questions are a foreground for the writing assignment and also echo some of the major themes of affirmative action: Just how far should we go to achieve equality?

4 HOW EQUAL ARE WE NOW?

Preparing to read (Student's Book pg. 134)

REVIEWING WHAT YOU HAVE ALREADY READ

This task is meant to bring together the ideas presented thus far in Chapter 6 and to launch the material in the final text and writing assignment. Encourage students to think about how the meaning of equality has changed since it was first named as a goal in the Declaration of Independence (See "All Men Are Created Equal," page 99 of the Student's Book.) and what various groups have done in their attempts to gain equality in our society. The text will give some information about their status today.

THINKING ABOUT THE TOPIC BEFORE YOU READ

The goal is for students to see that there have been many successes in minority communities. However, you should make it clear that minorities still face challenges.

Now read

Refer to page xi of this Teacher's Manual for suggestions about ways in which students can read the text.

➡ Remind students to review and update their vocabulary notebooks.

After you read (Student's Book pg. 137)

Task 1 UNDERSTANDING STATISTICS

1 | This task may be somewhat challenging because the information is not presented in order, some information must be inferred, and some boxes will have to remain blank because the information is not provided in the text. This task can be done individually or in pairs.

	Percentage that . . .	1970	1980	2000
African Americans	graduated from high school		51	79
	graduated from college		8	14
	lived in poverty			25
	owned a home			43
Latinos	graduated from high school	32		52
	graduated from college	4.5		11
	lived in poverty			25
	own a home			46
Whites	graduated from high school			89
	graduated from college			24
	lived in poverty			8
	owned a home			75

2 | Answers will vary but will probably include the idea that some progress has been made, but there are still differences between the economic status of the white majority and that of minorities. There is every reason to believe that both the progress and the gap will continue. As for progress, students may cite new laws, affirmative action, and changes in attitudes.

Task 2 BUILDING VOCABULARY: SYNONYMS

1 | These are high-frequency words that students tend to overuse. Learning synonyms for words they use often can make their writing more interesting and sophisticated.

Answers

1 big: large, considerable, substantial

2 a lot: substantially, considerably, significantly

3 go up: grew, has risen, has increased

2 | **Sample answers**
  - There has been considerable progress in improving the economic status of African Americans.
  - There are significantly more minorities in government than there were 30 years ago.
  - The high school graduation rate for Latinos increased from 32 percent to 52 percent between 1970 and 2000.

Task 3 LANGUAGE FOCUS: USING THE VERB *ESTIMATE* IN THE PASSIVE TO REPORT STATISTICS

1 | These phrases with *estimate* are extremely useful and relatively easy to use, even for beginning academic writers.

2 | **Sample answers**
  - It is estimated that only 12 percent of Hispanics earn more than $75,000 per year.
  - It is estimated that 40 percent of the white population earns more than $75,000 per year.

Task 4 THINKING CRITICALLY ABOUT THE TOPIC

This task allows students to demonstrate uniquely held knowledge and helps prepare them for the writing assignment, which will ask their view about accommodations for groups that have not received equal treatment in the past. Students may want to take notes during this discussion in anticipation of that assignment.

UNIT 3 WRITING ASSIGNMENT B

Preparing to write (Student's Book pg. 139)

1,2,
3 | Students should gather all of the notes they have collected as part of their work in this chapter. They can consult the notes during the discussion and as they consider their position and decide what group they wish to write about. Essentially, students are being asked to decide between the second and third interpretations of equality introduced at the beginning of this chapter, on page 120. The third is the argument on which affirmative action is based.

Now write

Remind students that academic writing generally does not use the first person. As a group, you may wish to generate some sentence frames that could substitute for the first person, such as *It is important for . . .* ; *The best solutions for . . . is . . .* ; *The government should . . .* ; and so on.

By now, students should be able to come up with a sentence on their own that states their claim. The rest of the assignment is laid out for them step by step, but make sure they understand what Choices A and B mean.

Sample papers

Choice A

The United States has taken many steps to make sure that all citizens are treated equally. However, because of a history of inequality, some groups still need some assistance to make sure that they are successful. It is fine to say that everyone starts out equal, but it is the government's job to ensure that they end up equal.

One group that needs extra help is the physically and mentally disabled. It is hard for them to do the same things that other people do. Some businesses do not want to hire them, and it is expensive to give them all the services they need. So, even though the law says they should be treated equally, this does not always happen.

The government needs to make sure that businesses and schools accommodate the disabled. If they do not, the government should punish the offenders with a fine. The disabled cannot always help themselves, so the government should take the responsibility to help them.

Choice B

Everyone is born more or less equal, and everyone has an equal chance for success. Your effort and ability will determine how successful you will be. If you become successful because of special treatment, then your success does not belong to you. People should depend on themselves and not on the government.

Many people believe that special treatment will help make society more equal and that special treatment can help correct a history of inequality. They say that in order to achieve complete equality, we must make sure that everyone gets equal access to resources, but we must also make sure that everyone is equally successful. This means that the people who try hard to succeed and the people who do not make a big effort end up the same. This is not fair, and it is not equality.

An equal society treats everyone the same. It is not fair to give special help to one specific group just because their parents or grandparents did not receive equal treatment. Success should depend on effort and merit.

After you write (Student's Book pg. 140)

1 | Make sure students give specific evidence for their feedback: What is the topic sentence? What is the evidence? If it is not persuasive, why not?

2 | Students can correct errors in grammar and spelling or simply circle errors for their partners to correct themselves. Remind them to check their list and add to it if need be.

American Values

Unit title page (Student's Book pg. 141)

Make sure students understand the meaning of the unit title. Ask them about their understanding of the term *values* and have them offer some values that they think are important in their own cultures.

Give students time to read the unit summary paragraph and check to be sure they understand the areas the unit will cover. Then ask them to look at the picture and think about how it relates to the unit, specifically Chapter 7.

Previewing the unit (Student's Book pg. 142)

Explain to students that the description and analysis of values presented in this unit represent generalizations that are not valid for all Americans or at every point in American history. Have students look at the pictures on this page and discuss what values they suggest.

Chapter 7: American Values from the Past

First have students identify the pictures (a farm, a factory, and a school) and what they represent; in other words, examine why these particular photographs were chosen for a unit on values. Then move on to the discussion question. Encourage students to discuss the factors in American economic and political success/dominance in the twentieth century. If the discussion is lively, you might follow it up with a question about whether its dominance is likely to continue and how this might (or might not) be related to those same values (or possibly the loss of them). This thread will be a focus of the chapter.

Chapter 8: American Values Today

This activity can be done in small groups or as a whole class. If you think the concepts presented in the list will be difficult for your students, you may want to opt for the latter. To check for comprehension, ask students for an example that illustrates each of the items. For example, many nineteenth-century immigrants illustrate the first point. Their belief in America as the land of opportunity is the reason they came.

Chapter 7

American Values from the Past

1 THE ROOTS OF AMERICAN VALUES

Preparing to read (Student's Book pg. 144)

INCREASING YOUR READING SPEED

1 | Make sure students review the strategies presented earlier in the book (Student's Book pg. 74).

2,3 | Remind students to omit the material in the box. Give them time to calculate their reading speed. Ask them what, if any, obstacles prevented them from reading more quickly (i.e., distractions, unknown words, etc.). Remind students to skip over unknown words unless they seem essential for comprehension.

4 | Make sure students understand that speed is useless without comprehension and they need to check that they have understood the text.

Answers

1 a, b, d, e, f, g, h

2 F a

T b

T c

F d

Now read

Refer to page xi of this Teacher's Manual for suggestions about ways in which students can read the text. Students can find another picture that includes Benjamin Franklin on page 1 of the Student's Book.

After you read (Student's Book pg. 147)

Task 1 BUILDING VOCABULARY: KEY TERMS

1 | These terms and concepts recur throughout the unit, so it is important that students understand them. They are recycled through several tasks.

Answers

1 self-discipline

2 optimism

3 individualism

4 values

5 risk

6 egalitarianism

7 self-reliance

2 | **Answers**

1 self-reliance

2 egalitarianism

3 risks (plural)

4 optimism

5 self-discipline

6 individualism

7 values

Task 2 THINKING ABOUT PROVERBS

1 | The meaning of some proverbs is not always transparent, so your students may need help understanding these. In particular, some vocabulary items may increase the difficulty level (e.g., *idle, can't stand, strokes, oaks, lemonade, will*).

2 | **Answers**

a	1
c	2
a	3
b, d	4
a, b	5
d	6
a, c	7
a, b	8
b	9
a, b, c	10

64 *Unit 4* American Values

3 | This is a good opportunity for sharing knowledge. Students can also draw parallels between the American proverbs and any proverbs they know from other cultures.

2 THE AMERICAN WEST

Preparing to read (Student's Book pg. 149)

THINKING ABOUT THE TOPIC BEFORE YOU READ

Students should recognize these familiar images, which they may have seen in films, books, games, or on television. Part of the goal of this chapter is to tease apart the romantic images that these media often portray and their roots in historical reality. This task begins this process. Ask students where they have seen images like these.

BUILDING VOCABULARY: PREVIEWING KEY TERMS

Students will need to understand these terms in order to comprehend the text.

Answers

1 frontier   **4** destiny

2 myth   **5** wilderness

3 pioneers

Now read

Refer to page xi of this Teacher's Manual for suggestions about ways in which students can read the text.

After you read (Student's Book pg. 152)

Task 1 READING TO FIND SUPPORT FOR MAIN IDEAS

1 | To a greater degree than in previous units, the texts in this unit are linked, so students may have to go back over material in previous texts in order to complete the tasks. Point out to your students that the need to synthesize as well as analyze is typical of academic work.

2 | This activity also recycles one of the note-taking strategies introduced earlier. Students may have already used this technique as they read.

Sample answers

Self-reliance:
- "Only the toughest and most self-reliant pioneers did well in these circumstances. They had to be able to build houses for themselves, farm, raise animals, hunt for food, and protect themselves and their property." (par. 3)

Optimism:
- "The land and the sky seemed to stretch without end, waiting for them. Many people also moved west to get away from the cities. They dreamed of a freer life in a wilder place." (par. 2)

Taking risks:
- "The journey west and life in the West were difficult. There were many physical hardships and few comforts or conveniences." (par. 3)

Egalitarianism:
- "A final important characteristic of the frontier was its social equality. In the struggle to survive, success depended on individual strength and resourcefulness, not on money or family background." (par. 3)

Task 2 THINKING CRITICALLY ABOUT THE TOPIC

Students' discussion should focus first on the romanticization of the past, and second, on the symbols and images that are related to primary values. For example, the log cabin might be related to self-reliance, the cowboy to independence, and the Wild West in general to optimism and endless bounty.

Task 3 READING PRIMARY TEXTS

1 | These entries contain difficult vocabulary words that are not crucial for students to understand. The point of this text is for students to get a flavor of the difficulty, danger, and sheer drudgery that accompanied the movement west. It was quite different than the journey often portrayed in popular media.

2 | Answers will vary but should include discussion of the hard work all pioneers had to do, the division of labor, and the lack of a childhood as we know it today.

3 | Again, answers will vary but should address the contrast between the romantic images on pages 145 and 149 of the Student's Book and the gritty reality of life in the western wilderness presented in the diary and images on page 151.

Task 4 LANGUAGE FOCUS: *FEW / A FEW*

1 | The similarity of these two quantifiers often causes confusion.

Answers
- "<u>Few</u> images have as powerful a place in the American imagination as the symbols of the American West, such as the covered wagon, the log cabin, and the cowboy." (par. 1)
- "There were many physical hardships and <u>few</u> comforts or conveniences." (par. 3)

2 | Students may note that the quantifier modifies something positive (comfort) and is linked to something negative (physical hardship).

Answer
Not many

3 | Students should notice the contrast between *sad* and *pleased*.

3 THE MARKETPLACE

Preparing to read (Student's Book pg. 154)

NOTE TAKING: USING A MAP

1 | This strategy for taking notes may be new to many students. It works well for visual learners who have some tolerance for ambiguity. Some students prefer the tighter structure of outlines. However, it is good for your students to try different methods to see what works best for them. Point out how the items in the circles are related to one another, how this method can be used to show looser relationships, and how it allows students to retain some flexibility in how they view the relationships among ideas.

2 | Students may want to add specific examples of businesses, business strategies, or examples of workers' rights issues.

Now read

Refer to page xi of this Teacher's Manual for suggestions about ways in which students can read the text.

After you read (Student's Book pg. 157)

Task 1 NOTE TAKING: CHECKING YOUR NOTES

1,2 | This will help students check the completeness of their note taking.

   1 innovative idea (risk taking), hard work

   2 machines replaced skilled workers; wages fell; work was dangerous

   3 lower wages, higher productivity ➞ higher profits

   4 national prosperity, national economic power

   5 lower wages, more competition for jobs

Task 2 BUILDING VOCABULARY: KEY TERMS

These are somewhat specialized, but still common, lexical items, many of which will reappear later in the text.

Answers

1 vertical integration   **2** monopoly   **3** trade union   **4** entrepreneur   **5** benefits

Task 3 BUILDING VOCABULARY: VERBS OF DIRECTION

1 | These are high-frequency verbs that are extremely useful in academic writing. Emphasize to students the importance of lexical variety and learning different ways of expressing the same ideas. Although the meaning of these verbs is clear, it can be confusing to sort out which are transitive, which are intransitive, and which can be both. The goal of this task is to make these distinctions clear.

Answers

Verb of direction	What went up or down?	Who/what controlled it?
reduce (par. 3)	competition	Carnegie
rise (par. 3)	profits	X
decrease (par. 4)	competition	Rockefeller
increase (par. 4)	profits	Rockefeller
decrease (par. 7)	wages	X
lower (par. 8)	profits	better pay for workers

2 | **Sample answers**
   - In the first half of the twentieth century, membership in trade unions rose.
   - The number of women and minorities in government office has increased considerably in the last 25 years.
   - After 1921, quotas reduced the number of immigrants from Asia.

4 EDUCATION FOR ALL

Preparing to read (Student's Book pg. 159)

BUILDING BACKGROUND KNOWLEDGE OF THE TOPIC

1 | Two of the words are glossed, but tell students not to worry too much about individual vocabulary items and instead, to try to get the gist.

2 | **Sample answers**
   1 Mann describes the difference in stark, and probably exaggerated, terms: In Europe, the upper class exploits the hard-working lower class. In Massachusetts, everyone has an equal chance to make a good living.

   2 **a** difficult to access, low quality; **b** easy to access, high quality

   3 toil, enjoy

   4 Answers will vary but should address the issue of access provided by education.

5 Answers will vary, but again, the connections to the values presented in the chapter should be clear. Education is an equalizer and is consistent with the idea that you will be rewarded for hard work and that class is not a barrier to success.

Now read

Refer to page xi of this Teacher's Manual for suggestions about ways in which students can read the text.

➡ Remind students to review and update their vocabulary notebooks.

After you read (Student's Book pg. 162)

Task 1 TEST TAKING: USING YOUR NOTES TO PREPARE

1,2 Emphasize to students that the choice of note-taking strategies is up to them and that they may find that different strategies fit different tasks and texts.

3 Students may wish to use a chart for this.

Sample answer

Reasons for public education: gets working-class children off the streets, educates the working class for citizenship, trains the labor force

4 This should help students see the utility of note taking, especially when they have heavier reading loads.

Sample answers to item 1
• What are some of the values on which public education is based?
• Why is a college education more important now than 50 years ago?
• What are some of the advantages of a college education?

Task 2 BUILDING VOCABULARY: WORDS THAT DESCRIBE TRENDS

Writing about trends is common in writing about the natural and social sciences. Stress to students that this high-frequency vocabulary is extremely useful.

1 **Answers**

People with more education <u>tend to</u> have better health, <u>are less likely to</u> become unemployed or go to prison, and <u>are more likely to</u> vote and participate in their community. The difference affects the next generation, too; children of college graduates <u>tend to</u> do better in school than children of high school graduates. Finally, children of college graduates are far <u>more likely to</u> complete their own college degree.

2 **Sample answers**

1 People with only a high school education <u>tend to have more health problems than college graduates</u>.

2 College graduates <u>tend to earn much more than people with just a high school education</u>.

3 People with a professional degree <u>are likely to earn twice as much as someone with just a college degree</u>.

4 <u>People with an education are more likely to</u> vote.

5 <u>The children of college graduates are more likely to</u> go to college.

3 | Answers will vary.

UNIT 4 WRITING ASSIGNMENT A

This writing assignment differs from the previous ones in that it begins in this chapter and is completed in the next one. As in past assignments, students are first asked to present their evidence (Chapter 7) and only later, to frame their argument more formally in an introduction (Chapter 8).

Preparing to write (Student's Book pg. 164)

In this step, students bring together all of the material in this chapter for consideration and evaluation. Emphasize that although the theme is their choice, they should choose one for which they have sufficient evidence to write a short paper.

Now write

In this assignment, there is still considerable guidance in shaping the paragraphs. However, this time students are expected to write their own topic sentence without the framing language provided in previous assignments. Because the introductory paragraph will be written in the next chapter, there is no need to worry about a formal claim or thesis statement at this time.

Sample paper (theme: hard work)

Hard work is an important theme in American business and economic success. Leaders in business who have worked hard to start and develop their businesses have often been very successful. Sometimes they have started with very little money. They just had a good idea and they were willing to work hard, even in jobs that were difficult and boring. Eventually the hard work led to success. We can see examples of this in the past, for example, Andrew Carnegie and John Rockefeller. Hard work is still important for success today, as we can see in the example of Sam Walton and Wal-Mart.

Hard work was also important in how the country was settled. The pioneers who moved west had few resources and worked hard on their farms and in towns. Their hard work brought prosperity to the West. Immigrants also contributed their hard work in factories, on railroads, and on farms. Today, many immigrants who come to the United States still hope that their hard work will bring them success.

After you write (Student's Book pg. 165)

As in previous assignments, the first section of "After you write" requires students to give concrete feedback by finding evidence for their partner's views. Later items (4 and 5) allow them to give more open-ended suggestions. For item 6, remind students that they should check the structures they chose to focus on in their writing in earlier chapters.

Chapter 8

American Values Today

1 THE INDIVIDUAL AND SOCIETY: RIGHTS AND RESPONSIBILITIES

Preparing to read (Student's Book pg. 166)

BUILDING VOCABULARY: PREVIEWING KEY TERMS

1, 2 | Remind students of the utility of predicting what the text will be about.

THINKING ABOUT THE TOPIC BEFORE YOU READ

This text contains material that is conceptually more difficult than some in other chapters. This discussion is an important one for setting the stage for your students' understanding, so it will be important for you to monitor them if they are talking in small groups. Alternatively, you could do this as a whole-class activity. Make sure the examples students are offering make sense within the context of the text they will read.

Now read

Refer to page xi of this Teacher's Manual for suggestions about ways in which students can read the text.

After you read (Student's Book pg. 169)

Task 1 VISUALIZING THE MAIN IDEAS

1 | Sometimes visual images are the most efficient way of explaining concepts. These two images illustrate the two basic tensions addressed in the text.

Answers

1 Individual rights versus the good of society

2 Self-reliance versus government support and assistance

2 | In this step, students must make the connection between a basic principle and examples offered in the text that support it. If the discussion in the "Preparing to read" section included relevant examples, add these as well.

Sample answers
- eminent domain
- New Deal

3 | If students have already brought up some examples in discussion, there is no need to review them. If they have used situations from outside of the United States, this presents a good opportunity to apply previous material to a new context.

Sample answers

Freedom of expression (Nazis marching, flag burning, etc.), affirmative action

Task 2 UNDERSTANDING THE FUNCTION OF DIFFERENT PARTS OF THE TEXT

This task should be familiar to students. Students are not asked to explain the function of the parts of the text, only to match them. This is a much easier task and should be within their grasp. You may want to follow this idea up in later texts to see if students can explain the functions of paragraphs that are relatively easy to identify.

Answers

_2_	**1**	_1_	**3**
_3–6_	**2**	_4, 7_	**4**

2 THE OPEN ROAD

Preparing to read (Student's Book pg. 170)

SCANNING

1 | **Answers**

1 fewer than 5 million	**3** 90 percent	**5** 90 percent
2 77 percent	**4** 42,000	**6** 200 million

2 | This is another reason to scan – it can help predict what a text will be about.

THINKING ABOUT THE TOPIC BEFORE YOU READ

This activity provides an opportunity for students to consider personal connections to the topic and to offer their own experiences. The second question foreshadows one of the main themes of the text: that cars are, and always have been, about more than transportation.

Now read

Refer to page xi of this Teacher's Manual for suggestions about ways in which students can read the text.

After you read (Student's Book pg. 173)

Task 1 THINKING CRITICALLY ABOUT THE TOPIC

1,2 | This task follows up on the theme introduced in "Preparing to read." Depending on your students' knowledge of American cars and American culture, they may mention the large size of many cars, their gas consumption, and the image-conscious but environmentally unfriendly SUV.

3 | If you have a heterogeneous classroom, responses may range from the relatively lower importance of private cars in students' cultures in which public transportation plays a greater role, to a discussion of places where cars may be a more important personal statement than homes.

Task 2 LANGUAGE FOCUS: *BECAUSE / BECAUSE OF*

1 | These are phonologically and semantically similar, but they differ in their grammatical role, which can easily cause confusion. It is more important for students to understand their function than their name.

Answers
- "First, the price of cars dropped significantly (because of) Henry Ford, an extremely successful entrepreneur." (par. 2)
- "Those who lived far from their jobs needed to drive (because) there was little public transportation from the suburbs to the city." (par. 3)
- "Today, the 'drive-through' or 'drive-up' is popular, not (because) people want to be in their cars, but because they want to save time." (boxed text)

2 | **Answers and sample answers**

1 religious persecution	**3** because of	**5** past discrimination
2 because	**4** they were opposed to integration	**6** because

3 THE TWENTY-FIRST-CENTURY MARKETPLACE

Preparing to read (Student's Book pg. 174)

SKIMMING
Remind students of the importance of skimming as a strategy for academic reading.

Answers

1 American business   **2** Google, Wal-Mart

THINKING ABOUT THE TOPIC BEFORE YOU READ
Students may differ considerably in their knowledge of these two businesses. You may have to provide some background information.

Now read

Refer to page xi of this Teacher's Manual for suggestions about ways in which students can read the text.

After you read (Student's Book pg. 177)

Task 1 READING FOR MAIN IDEAS

1 | This task is best done individually.

Sample answers

1 good education

2 hard work

3 understanding of the business world/technology

2 | **Sample answers**

1 putting most popular results first   **2** discounting

3 | **Sample answers**

variety, low prices, convenience of being able to buy many products in one store

Task 2 READING FOR DETAILS

Once students are sure of the main ideas, it is easier for them to focus on details. Remind them that details play an important role in building arguments, and they are often needed in writing assignments.

Answers

	Google	Wal-Mart
1. started with a good idea	✓	✓
2. pioneered new business practices	✓	✓
3. began in a garage with borrowed money	✓	
4. uses computer technology	✓	✓
5. can help you find a date	✓	
6. has been very successful	✓	✓
7. has many stores		✓
8. is used more than 200 million times a day	✓	
9. offers services in many languages	✓	

Task 3 LANGUAGE FOCUS: *SO . . . THAT / SUCH . . . THAT*

1 These are often called degree complements. There are many different kinds – more than the number shown here – and this task is just an introduction. It is not expected that students will master this structure here.

Answers

1 <u>He bought products in</u> such large quantities that <u>he could demand very low prices from his suppliers</u> . . . (par. 4)

2 . . . <u>he built enormous stores that sold everything from toys to light bulbs at</u> such low prices that <u>smaller stores could not compete</u>. (par. 4)

3 <u>Wal-Mart was</u> so successful that <u>Sam Walton became one of the richest men in the country</u>. (par. 4)

2 Sample answers

1 Google works so well that <u>it has become the most popular search engine</u>.

2 Wal-Mart's prices are so <u>low</u> that <u>it is difficult for other stores to compete</u>.

3 If this is students' first exposure to the structure, don't expect them to complete this step without errors. Answers will vary.

4 IS THE AMERICAN DREAM STILL POSSIBLE?

Preparing to read (Student's Book pg. 179)

CONDUCTING A SURVEY

1 This activity should be fun as well as informative. This chapter ties up the themes of values and the American Dream, and this task lets students give their own input. This step could be done before students open their books and have a chance to look at the categories used by the *New York Times*, which are described in the chart in step 2.

2 Students can conduct this survey in class or, if you wish, they can conduct it outside of class as a homework assignment. If you are in an EFL classroom, the students obviously will have to translate the questions into their native language.

3 If your students are good at using Excel, they can create a graph from their results. If not, percentages will work just as well.

Now read

Refer to page xi of this Teacher's Manual for suggestions about ways in which students can read the text.

➡ Remind students to review and update their vocabulary notebooks.

After you read (Student's Book pg. 182)

Task 1 EXAMINING GRAPHIC MATERIAL

1 | This task requires students to do more than just read answers off the graph, so warn them that some interpretation will be needed.

Answers

<u>T</u> **1**   <u>F</u> **2**   <u>T</u> **3**   <u>T</u> **4**   <u>F</u> **5**

2 | **Sample answers**
   - Most people say that education is important or essential for success.
   - Only about 10 percent of the respondents said that a wealthy family is an essential factor in getting ahead.

3 | This activity will work well as a class discussion.

Task 2 WRITING DEFINITIONS: THE XYZ FORMAT

1,2 | This task recycles the first writing assignment.

Sample answers

1 A *meritocracy* is a system that rewards effort and talent.

2 A *property tax* is a tax that is based on the value of property.

3 A *consumer nation* is a country that consumes more than it produces.

Task 3 WRITING DEFINITIONS: USING *MEAN* + A GERUND

1 | The XYZ format is not the only way to write a definition. The gerund form is more informal and is characteristic of spoken language.

Answer

"Some say it means <u>having freedom and living in a society based on equality</u>; however, most think it means <u>achieving economic security and success</u>. In other words, the American Dream means <u>having upward economic and social mobility</u> . . ." (par. 1)

2 | **Sample answers**

1 Upward economic and social mobility means improving your financial and social situation.

2 Optimism means feeling positive about the future.

3 Success means getting ahead.

4 Freedom of expression means being able to say what you believe.

5 Self-discipline means making yourself do important things even when you don't want to.

6 Vertical integration means controlling all aspects of an industry.

Task 4 UNDERSTANDING THE USES OF PARENTHESES

Parentheses are used in various ways, and often their meaning is implicit.

Answers

Chapter and text	Passage from the text	Purpose of parentheses		
		extra information	**definition**	**source or date of source**
Ch. 7, Text 1 (page 146)	1. *Benjamin Franklin (1706–1790)*	✓		
Ch. 7, Text 2 (page 151)	2. *Still in camp, husband and myself being sick (caused we supposed by drinking the river water).*	✓		
Ch. 7, Text 3 (page 156)	3. *Industries that are controlled almost entirely by one company, such as the steel industry (controlled mainly by Carnegie's company) and the oil industry (controlled mainly by Rockefeller's company) are called monopolies.*	✓		
Ch. 8, Text 1 (page 168)	4. *An important example of the need to balance self-reliance and government assistance is the federal government's response to the problems of the Great Depression (1929–1940).*	✓		
Ch. 8, Text 2 (page 171)	5. *One example of this is the popular SUV (sport-utility vehicle).*		✓	
Ch. 8, Text 4 (page 181)	6. *A 1978 survey found that 23 percent of adult men from the bottom fifth of the population (in social and economic terms) had moved to the top fifth . . . .*	✓		
	7. *The* New York Times *(2005)*			✓

UNIT 4 WRITING ASSIGNMENT B

Preparing to write (Student's Book pg. 185)

1,2 | This assignment builds on the writing done in the last chapter. Some of the information presented in the chapter may be useful in supporting the arguments that students made in the last writing assignment. They should go back and review what they wrote after the last chapter.

Now write

This assignment addresses the introductory paragraph. Students must include three elements: (1) a general introduction to the topic, (2) a thesis statement (though that terminology is not used here), and (3) an explanation of what will be in the rest of the paper.

1 | In this first step, students must write a general introduction to the topic.

2 | Thesis statements are difficult to write, even for competent writers. In this assignment, a great deal of linguistic and content support is provided, but this is a more autonomous task than previous writing assignments in which the thesis was provided.

3 | Again, a great deal of linguistic support is provided. Students may want to go back and review their Chapter 7 writing assignments first.

4 | Encourage your students to revise their earlier assignments to include any new information from this chapter. Emphasize that good writers revise all the time and that to rewrite is by no means a sign of failure or lack of skill.

5 | It may be useful to put this graphic on an overhead if students are writing in class.

Sample introductory paragraph

key:
[general introduction] in brackets
<u>thesis statement</u> underlined
(explanation of what will be in the rest of the paper) in parentheses

[Every culture has a set of beliefs that guides behavior and attitudes. There are many specific values and beliefs that relate to American history and culture.] <u>Many aspects of American culture are based on the value of hard work.</u> (Hard work has played an extremely important role in the development of American business and was also an important factor in the settlement of the American West.)

After you write (Student's Book pg. 186)

1 | Peer feedback is beneficial, but students must learn to do their own revising and editing. At this stage, it is still useful for them to have explicit guidelines for doing so. If students are doing a cursory job of this, ask them to locate and identify each of these elements.

2 | Students should be making a list and adding to it with each assignment. They should check the new grammar item as well as the ones they have chosen in the past.

3 | If students have identified the key elements in their own writing, it may be useful to see if their peers can do so with the same outcome. Students should provide clean copies to their classmates so that the peer editor will not be biased by a copy that has been marked up by the writer.

Spotlight on Culture

Unit **5**

Unit title page (Student's Book pg. 187)

Ask students to look at the photo collage and think about how it relates to the unit title.

Give students time to read the unit summary paragraph and check to make sure they understand the areas the unit will cover.

Previewing the unit (Student's Book pg. 188)

Although the focus on globalization is not until Chapter 10, it is important that students understand the concept from the outset. A brief discussion on the connection between culture and globalization before beginning the unit may avoid confusion later.

Chapter 9: American Innovations

1 | You may want to offer one or two more examples and then ask for suggestions from individual students.

2 | Some of the answers may surprise your students. Answers are at the bottom of the Student's Book page.

Chapter 10: Global Transformations

1 | If you have not yet discussed the concept of globalization, you will need to do so now. Encourage your students to think of other examples beyond the photographs on page 187.

2 | This question has two parts to allow all students to contribute their knowledge and experience. It may be that only one part is appropriate for your class.

American Innovations

1 AMERICA'S MUSIC: THE BLUES AND JAZZ

Preparing to read (Student's Book pg. 190)

THINKING ABOUT THE TOPIC BEFORE YOU READ

These forms of music may not be familiar to all of your students, but there are usually a few students who have some knowledge of either the blues or jazz. It may be useful to have them look at the photos on page 191. Let students share their knowledge with their classmates. If no one volunteers, you will have to be ready to provide some background. If you have access to a CD player, the best course is to play some samples of the music.

READING PRIMARY TEXTS

1 | This text contains some difficult vocabulary, but it is fun and worth students' trouble. There is no need to make them struggle to figure out the words in context. Just explain any words they don't know.

2 | The point of these questions is twofold: (1) Students should infer the author's negative opinion, which is based on some connection between the music and sex, although you need not be that explicit; and (2) Students, especially young people, can apply these ideas to their own experiences and their own music.

Now read

Refer to page xi of this Teacher's Manual for suggestions about ways in which students can read the text.

After you read (Student's Book pg. 193)

Task 1 NOTE TAKING: USING A CHART

This task gives students another chance to practice the skill. It can be done individually or in pairs.

Sample answers

Par.	Topic	Details
1	intro – importance of blues and jazz	• influence on soul, rock, rap, and classical • major artists who use jazz
2	origins of blues	• slavery • meaning of blues: about loss and pain
3	origins of jazz	• where: in the South • when: beginning of 20th century
4	jazz style	• connection to blues • unique elements: • emphasizes individual musicians • spontaneous performance
5	social importance	• race relations • mixed audiences • mixed bands
6	jazz and society	• racial inequality • comparison to democracy

Task 2 TEST TAKING: USING YOUR NOTES TO PREPARE

1 | Give students time to review the material about test questions on page 110.

2 | **Sample answers**
   • Analyze how the blues and jazz are related to each other.
   • Describe the origins of the blues and jazz.
   • Compare and contrast the blues and jazz.

3 | Give students time to answer their partner's questions. This should be done orally – they aren't expected to answer the questions in writing.

Task 3 BUILDING VOCABULARY: SYNONYMS

This text contains similar ideas expressed with different words. Make sure students understand that the responses need two words; that is, they need to include the appropriate preposition.

Answers

1 roots in

2 links to

3 impact on

Task 4 THINKING CRITICALLY ABOUT THE TOPIC

1,2 | The discussion should include the idea that this musical style not only provides the opportunity for individual autonomy and performance, but also requires collaboration in order for the group to be successful.

2 HOLLYWOOD AND THE MOVIES

Preparing to read (Student's Book pg. 195)

THINKING ABOUT THE TOPIC BEFORE YOU READ

1 | The syntax of this quotation is a little difficult, so make sure students understand that *cut out* means "removed."

2 | Discussion should include the idea of cinema as escape and adventure.

3 | Responses will vary depending on the ages of your students and their exposure to American popular culture. These images are from examples of three of Hollywood's most popular film genres: the romantic comedy (left), the gangster movie (right), and the Western (below). You may have to provide some background information.

Now read

Refer to page xi of this Teacher's Manual for suggestions about ways in which students can read the text.

After you read (Student's Book pg. 197)

Task 1 ASKING AND ANSWERING QUESTIONS ABOUT A TEXT

1 | Remind students that this is a useful strategy for promoting comprehension and preparing for written assignments.

Answers to item 2

a new technology and business practices

b movies provided escape; contrast with the hardships of the Depression

c a shared cultural experience, sent American culture worldwide

d around 1950; television

2 | Give students time to explain all the answers.

Task 2 TEST TAKING: WRITING A SUMMARY FROM YOUR NOTES TO PREPARE

1 | Writing a summary is one of the more difficult academic tasks. It will take many attempts for your students to get good at it. This semi-structured task is a good transition to independent writing.

2 | **Sample answer**

Hollywood's Golden Age, or the time when American movies were most popular, lasted from the 1920s through the 1950s. Hollywood studios were powerful then because of new technology and vertical integration. The Golden Age was a time when people all over the world shared the experience of seeing movies. This helped people forget the Great Depression.

3 | You may want to do this as a class on an overhead transparency.

3 AMERICAN SPORTS

Preparing to read (Student's Book pg. 198)

THINKING ABOUT THE TOPIC BEFORE YOU READ

Ask your students if they watch or play any of the sports represented by the balls. Do they follow any American sports teams? Answers appear on the bottom of the Student's Book page.

Now read

Refer to page xi of this Teacher's Manual for suggestions about ways in which students can read the text.

After you read (Student's Book pg. 201)

Task 1 READING FOR DETAILS

Be sure students are aware of the negative – which detail is NOT supported by the text.

Answers

_b_	**1**	_b_	**5**
_c_	**2**	_c_	**6**
_b_	**3**	_a_	**7**
_b_	**4**		

Task 2 THINKING ABOUT CULTURE-SPECIFIC EXPRESSIONS

1 | We use sports metaphors and terms all the time. The difference with these is they have been divorced from their original sports context and are now part of everyday speech. You may think of some others that you can share. Students may offer some from sports they are familiar with.

2 | **Answers**

  1 touch base   4 struck out

  2 on the ball   5 ballpark

  3 out of left field   6 right off the bat

Task 3 CREATING A GRAPH FROM A SURVEY

1 | Moving from textual to graphic information is an important skill to master. This task practices this skill with new content and a little fun.

2 | The survey can be done in class or assigned as homework with data to be collected in students' communities.

3 | The chart can be a simple bar graph, as shown, or something more complicated if the students wish.

Task 4 THINKING CRITICALLY ABOUT THE TOPIC

Students may not have given sports much serious thought, but in fact, the sociology of sports is an active academic discipline. The discussion need not cover all of these questions. Focus on aspects of the topic that seem to be of most interest to your students.

4 THE DEVELOPMENT AND IMPACT OF THE INTERNET

Preparing to read (Student's Book pg. 204)

THINKING ABOUT THE TOPIC BEFORE YOU READ

1,2 | Filling in the chart should not take up much time. It is just supposed to get students thinking about the topic as it relates to their own lives. They may have activities to add, but that can wait until step 3.

3 | For younger students, going back 10 years may be a stretch. You may have to offer your own experience.

Now read

Refer to page xi of this Teacher's Manual for suggestions about ways in which students can read the text.

➡ Remind students to review and update their vocabulary notebooks.

After you read (Student's Book pg. 207)

Task 1 BUILDING VOCABULARY: KEY TERMS

1 | **Answers**

<u>b</u> **1**   <u>e</u> **4**

<u>c</u> **2**   <u>d</u> **5**

<u>a</u> **3**

2 | Give students a few minutes to compare answers.

Task 2 EXAMINING GRAPHIC MATERIAL

1,2 | At the end of the task, if there is time, you may want to discuss the significance of the digital divide, both in the United States and across the world. If time is short, this can be incorporated into the next task (item 3).

Sample answers

1 Asian Americans are more likely to have Internet access.

2 People with high incomes tend to have Internet access.

3 People who are highly educated are more likely to have Internet access than people who never went to college.

Task 3 THINKING CRITICALLY ABOUT THE TOPIC

Sample answers

1 easy information exchange and access; cheap publication

2 security problems, access to dangerous information, chains us to work, spread of lies and hate speech

3 Discussion should include the impact of the digital divide between rich and poor, less and more educated, and their access to the Internet.

4 Discussion should include the notion of relatively cheap access to information and greater participation across national, class, and community boundaries.

UNIT 5 WRITING ASSIGNMENT A

In step 4, students are asked to use outside sources for the first time in this short assignment. This need not be a major part of the assignment, or included at all, if you think they are not ready. If you do include it, make sure students have some understanding of how to incorporate outside sources without copying.

Preparing to write (Student's Book pg. 209)

1,2 | Check students' choices before they begin to write. Some choices may lend themselves to the assignment more easily than others. The innovation should be a fairly substantial item, and not, for example, a national dish.

3 | You may want to join each group for a few minutes as they discuss their choices.

4 | This step depends on the availability of the Internet and other resources and is really up to you. It is possible that students will need guidance in doing the research. You may want to suggest a limited number of sites or references. However, depending on your class, it is possible that your students will be more familiar with resources than you are, especially Internet sources. Whatever you decide, limit the number of sources that students consult. The assignment is more about the writing than the research.

Now write

The first paragraph should be general, simply stating that the innovation is an important one and giving some background information. The reasons for its importance should be developed in the second paragraph.

Sample paper

The elevator is an important modern innovation. The first elevators did not use electricity; they used ropes pulled by humans, and later, water power. However, their importance grew considerably with the use of electricity. Today, most modern buildings depend on elevators to take people to different floors quickly and easily.

Elevators have become necessary in the modern world because we have lots of tall buildings, and people have to be able to get to the high floors. So, elevators have made it possible for us to have skyscrapers. They have allowed us to build higher and higher and create communities where thousands of people live and work close together. Some scholars say the elevator is the innovation that made it possible to have modern cities.

After you write (Student's Book pg. 210)

1,2 | This time, students are left to figure out revision strategies for themselves. If they are having difficulty, they can review previous "After you write" sections or consult step 3 of this one.

3,4, | These steps are addressed to peers, but could as easily be used by the writers
5 | themselves.

Global Transformations

1 GLOBAL CHANGES AND IMPROVEMENTS TO AMERICAN INNOVATIONS

Preparing to read (Student's Book pg. 211)

BUILDING VOCABULARY: PREVIEWING KEY TERMS

1 | Students can consult an online dictionary such as the *Cambridge Advanced Learner's Dictionary* at www.dictionary.cambridge.org.

2 | If necessary, have students consult the task on making definitions with *mean* + a gerund on page 183 of the Student's Book.

Sample answers

1 Adopting an innovation means starting to use it.

2 Adapting an innovation means changing it to fit a new context.

3 Developing an innovation means changing it to make it better or bigger.

3 | Check that students are able to come up with an example.

Now read

Refer to page xi of this Teacher's Manual for suggestions about ways in which students can read the text.

After you read (Student's Book pg. 214)

Task 1 READING FOR MAIN IDEAS

1 | **Sample answers**

    1 cellular phone technology

    2 animation

    3 baseball

2 | **Sample answers**

    • The technique of film animation, which began in the United States, was very influential. For example, it was an important influence in the development of *anime* in Japan.

    • Baseball, which started in the United States, is now very popular in other countries, such as Japan and the Dominican Republic.

Task 2 LANGUAGE FOCUS: *UNTIL / NOT . . . UNTIL*

1 | **Answers**

    1 they are 18 years old

    2 1870 / the passage of the Fifteenth Amendment

    3 1954

    4 men returned from the war

    5 the 1950s

    6 Snowboarding / 1998

2 | **Sample answers**

    • Immigration quotas continued until 1965.

    • Significant numbers of African Americans did not begin voting until the passage of the Voting Rights Act in 1965.

2 FAST FOOD

Preparing to read (Student's Book pg. 215)

THINKING ABOUT THE TOPIC BEFORE YOU READ

This should be a familiar topic to students, and most have something to say about it, good or bad.

PREVIEWING ART IN THE TEXT

Students should make the connections between the health risks of smoking and eating fast food.

Now read

Refer to page xi of this Teacher's Manual for suggestions about ways in which students can read the text.

After you read (Student's Book pg. 218)

Task 1 NOTE TAKING: USING A GRAPHIC ORGANIZER

Some texts lend themselves more easily to graphic representation than others. "Fast Food" illustrates causes and consequences and works well with this technique.

1 | Give students time to review the text.

Sample answers

Reasons for increase in FF   Effects of increase in FF
Need for convenience   Fewer meals at home
Need to save time   → | Increase in FF
restaurants | →   Changes in diet
                                                Health problems

2 | **Sample answer**

Students might add a box to the diagram to follow Increase in FF restaurants.
Increase in FF restaurants → Health problems → changes in FF menus

Task 2 BUILDING VOCABULARY: USING GRAMMAR AND CONTEXT TO GUESS UNKNOWN WORDS

1 | Emphasize that there are often many clues in the surrounding text that may help students guess meaning. These include both grammatical clues and other words in context. Students may need some initial assistance utilizing the clues in the last column.

Answers

1 noun   4 adjective

2 adjective   5 noun

3 noun   6 adjective

2 | **Answers**

1 choices

2 quick and easy to eat and/or prepare

3 Eating fast food is not the only reason for the national weight problem.

4 fat; fatness or the state of being fat

5 don't get enough exercise

Task 3 EXAMINING GRAPHIC MATERIAL

1 | This task is a little different than others in the text. Students may not be expecting to do calculations in a reading-writing textbook. Nevertheless, this is not unusual in academic texts, particularly in the social sciences.

2 | Discussion should include the health risks of fast food (fat, sodium, and calories).

Task 4 THINKING CRITICALLY ABOUT THE TOPIC
You may wish to remind students of the discussion about individual versus government rights and responsibilities in Unit 4. This discussion may be done as a whole class.

3 HIP-HOP: THE CULTURE AND THE MUSIC

Preparing to read (Student's Book pg. 221)

THINKING ABOUT THE TOPIC BEFORE YOU READ
Depending on your class, how much students have to say can vary greatly. Ask those who know this music well to talk about rap musicians from their own communities.

Now read

Refer to page xi of this Teacher's Manual for suggestions about ways in which students can read the text.

After you read (Student's Book pg. 224)

Task 1 READING FOR MAIN IDEAS AND DETAILS
Remind students to base their answers only on information in the text, and not on any knowledge they may have had prior to reading it.

Answers

D	1	M	6
M	2	D	7
M	3	D	8
NI	4	D	9
D	5	NI	10

Task 2 LANGUAGE FOCUS: USING EVEN AS AN ADVERB
Even is one of those words that native speakers use all the time but is rarely explained in course books.

1,2 | **Answers**
 1 The popularity of drive-in theaters versus drive-in restaurants and the speed and risk of extreme sports versus traditional sports are being compared.

 2 Most music performance is expensive, and rap is not. We might not expect music in a language without sound.

3 | **Answers**
  U 1 U 2 C 3 U 4 C 5

4 | **Sample answers**

1 Overlap between rap and classical music is unexpected, so this is a surprise.

2 Factory workers generally could not afford to buy cars, so this is a surprise.

3 His profits in the future would be higher than before, so this is a comparison.

4 One would expect that success in the retail business would be based on a great product, so the fact that Walton had none is a surprise.

5 This rate of population growth is compared to previous years.

5 | Answers will vary.

4 ENGLISH AS A GLOBAL LANGUAGE

Preparing to read (Student's Book pg. 226)

THINKING ABOUT THE TOPIC BEFORE YOU READ
Be sure that students understand the distinction between cause and result. If they grasp this, reading the text will become much easier, and, as a result, their reading speed will increase. Answers are at the bottom of the Student's Book page.

INCREASING YOUR READING SPEED
When students have finished, have them turn back to the first "Increasing your reading speed" task (Student's Book page 74) to see how much their speed has increased.

Now read

Refer to page xi of this Teacher's Manual for suggestions about ways in which students can read the text.

➡ Remind students to review and update their vocabulary notebooks.

After you read (Student's Book pg. 229)

Task 1 LANGUAGE FOCUS: NOUN + INFINITIVE PHRASES

1 | Learning chunks like this instead of single words is a good way for students to improve their academic writing.

Answers
1 "As more and more communication occurs in English, the (need) to learn English has increased."

2 "Finally, the political and economic cost of losing the (ability) to understand one another is just too high."

1 All people should have an equal (chance) to succeed.

2 The Constitution gives Congress the (power) to create courts.

3 It seemed to be a land of endless opportunity for someone with a good idea and the (willingness) to take a risk.

4 The Nineteenth Amendment gave women the (right) to vote.

5 Many settlers believed it was their (destiny) to populate the land from one coast to the other.

6 The Japanese are developing a (way) to pay by using a cell phone.

7 A car meant the (freedom) to come and go wherever you wanted.

3 | **Sample answers**

1 Many Americans believe they have a right to own a gun.

2 The government has a responsibility to help those who cannot help themselves.

Task 2 EXAMINING GRAPHIC MATERIAL

Make sure students understand that this graph pertains to young people and not to the general population.

1 | **Answers**

1 Arabic

2 growing population, increase in importance

3 Chinese

4 falling birth rate

2 | When students have answered the questions, you may want to segue into the next discussion by asking if/how these figures impact the future of global English.

Task 3 THINKING CRITICALLY ABOUT THE TOPIC

1 | If any of your students are from countries where English functions as a second language, you can have them offer examples of how English is used there.

2 | This step can be done in small groups or as a whole class.

3 | These questions bring together many of the ideas addressed throughout Chapter 10. Encourage students to focus on the balance between influence and dominance.

UNIT 5 WRITING ASSIGNMENT B

In this assignment, students again have the option of doing outside research.

Preparing to write (Student's Book pg. 232)

Although students may be eager to talk about a particular innovation, it is important to stress that this paper is a vehicle for an argument about globalization. It is not just a description of the innovation itself.

Now write

Good preparation is key in successful writing. It would be useful to check the choices your students have made to see if they fit the assignment. Is it an innovation? Where has it moved? Has it changed in some important way?

Sample paper

The globalization of popular culture is a reality today. Many elements of culture, such as music, fashion, and even language, have crossed national and community borders. As soon as something becomes popular in one country, it jumps to another country. Usually it is changed at least a little bit in the new country or culture, and sometimes it returns to the original country in that new form. One example of popular culture that started in the United States and has traveled around the world is the soap opera.

Soap operas began on the radio in the United States in the 1930s and later crossed into many different countries. The word *soap* comes from the soap companies that paid for advertising in the early days of the shows. The shows are drama programs that continue without end. They have many characters and are usually about the home and love lives of these characters, which are very dramatic and filled with problems. There are crimes and bad behavior. Soap operas moved to daytime television in the 1950s.

Today, soap operas are popular all over the world. They are especially popular in Latin America, where they are called *telenovelas*, and in Korea. In Latin America, *telenovelas* are a multimillion-dollar industry. *Telenovelas* have become popular all over the world, even among people who do not speak Spanish. Some of the stars, such as Salma Hayek, have become American movie stars, and some of the programs, such as *Betty la Fea* (*Ugly Betty*), have been adapted for American television. South Korea also has a very active soap opera industry. Some programs are similar to American soap operas; for example, they may show the lives of doctors and nurses. Others, such as *Jewel in the Palace*, are historical. The shows also have fans all over the world, from China to the United States. Soap operas show universal human emotions and situations. Therefore, they can cross national and cultural boundaries and find audiences everywhere.

After you write (Student's Book pg. 233)

If you have not been asking for a second draft, it would be a good idea to do so before the course ends. Although teachers in most academic classes will not require multiple drafts, it is important for learners to understand the value of revising and get into the habit of doing so.

Unit **1** CONTENT QUIZ

PART 1 True/False questions (24 points)

Decide if the following statements are true (T) or false (F).

_____ **1** The President of the United States writes the country's laws.

_____ **2** The United States government is prohibited from supporting any particular religion.

_____ **3** The President of the United States is directly elected by the people.

_____ **4** Almost 50 percent of Americans own guns.

_____ **5** After the War of Independence, Americans wanted a strong central government.

_____ **6** The Supreme Court is part of the judicial branch of government.

PART 2 Multiple choice questions (24 points)

Circle the best answer from the choices listed.

1 Which of the following factors does *not* explain why settlers came to the American colonies?
   a for religious freedom
   b to escape from war
   c for greater social equality
   d for economic opportunity

2 The First Amendment to the Constitution guarantees
   a the privacy of all citizens.
   b protection for people accused of crimes.
   c the right to own a gun.
   d freedom of religion.

3 Only the federal government, and not state governments,
   a controls the military.
   b collects taxes.
   c makes laws for business.
   d pays for schools.

4 In colonial America, militias were originally formed to
   a hunt wild animals and provide food.
   b protect the settlers.
   c fight wars.
   d support the Constitution.

PART 3 Short answer questions (24 points)

In one or two sentences, write a short answer to each of the following questions.

1 What is a *federalist* system of government?

2 What is the difference between the electoral vote and the popular vote?

3 What is the purpose of the Bill of Rights?

PART 4 One paragraph answer (28 points)

Choose one of the following topics and write a paragraph about it. Use a separate sheet of paper.

1 The system of checks and balances is a fundamental part of the American government.

2 There are some important limits on freedom of speech in the United States.

Unit **2** CONTENT QUIZ

PART 1 True/False questions (24 points)

Decide if the following statements are true (T) or false (F).

_____ **1** The average life of a slave was half as long as the average life of a white person.

_____ **2** Today the largest number of immigrants comes from Mexico and India.

_____ **3** Immigrants who arrived in the United States in the last half of the nineteenth century found jobs quickly and easily.

_____ **4** Whites are now a minority in the United States.

_____ **5** The grandchildren of most immigrants to the United States speak English as their first language.

_____ **6** Most illegal immigrants in the United States come from Mexico.

PART 2 Multiple choice questions (24 points)

Circle the best answer from the choices listed.

1 The *triangular trade* involved
  a Africa, Portugal, and the American colonies.
  b Africa, South America, and North America.
  c Africa, the Caribbean, and cities in North America.
  d the Caribbean, New York, and London.

2 In the eighteenth century, the largest number of immigrants to the United States came from
  a southern and eastern Europe.
  b China and Japan.
  c Canada and Mexico.
  d western Europe.

3 The highest rate of increase of Latinos in the United States in the last decade has been
  a in the southeast: Georgia, South Carolina, and North Carolina.
  b in the large cites on the coasts.
  c in California.
  d in the southwest: New Mexico, Arizona, and Texas.

4 One important part of the government's policy of assimilation of Native Americans was
  a a series of treaties with native tribes.
  b the removal of 4,000 Cherokee to Oklahoma.
  c the establishment of reservations.
  d boarding schools where native children learned white culture.

PART 3 Short answer questions (24 points)

In one or two sentences, write a short answer to each of the following questions.

1 Name three factors that contributed to the destruction of Native American communities.

2 What are two arguments against the continued high rate of immigration to the United States?

3 Name three groups of people who profited from slavery.

PART 4 One paragraph answer (28 points)

Choose one of the following topics and write a paragraph about it. Use a separate sheet of paper.

1 Immigrants have not always been welcomed in the United States.

2 Illegal immigration to the United States is likely to continue.

Unit **3** CONTENT QUIZ

PART 1 True/False questions (24 points)

Decide if the following statements are true (T) or false (F).

_____ **1** Jim Crow laws prevented many Southern blacks from voting.

_____ **2** Discrimination against African Americans ended when the Civil Rights Act of 1964 became law.

_____ **3** Many people with disabilities have low education levels and low incomes.

_____ **4** The percentages of African Americans, Latinos, and whites who are poor are now almost equal.

_____ **5** Today, American women marry at a later age than they did in 1960.

_____ **6** Women and blacks were excluded from statements about equality in the Declaration of Independence and the Constitution.

PART 2 Multiple choice questions (24 points)

Circle the best answer from the choices listed.

1 *Brown versus Board of Education of Topeka* was a court case that
   a gave equal voting rights to African Americans.
   b integrated buses and trains in the American South.
   c ended segregation in schools.
   d settled the boycott of buses in Alabama.

2 The goal of affirmative action is to
   a guarantee equal treatment for all people.
   b help the best students get into good universities.
   c help poor people get ahead.
   d achieve equal outcomes.

3 Since the 1960s, women have achieved many goals in their fight for equality. One goal they have *not* achieved is
   a equal pay for equal work.
   b equal representation in colleges and universities.
   c greater representation in government.
   d more equal division of labor at home.

4 Until the 1960s, discrimination against African Americans was
   a practiced only in the South.
   b based on the Thirteenth Amendment.
   c a result of the Civil War.
   d accepted throughout the country.

PART 3 Short answer questions (24 points)

In one or two sentences, write a short answer to each of the following questions.

1 Name two ways to measure the equality of different groups in addition to their educational level.

2 Name three barriers that prevented African Americans from voting after amendments to the Constitution gave them the right to vote.

3 Name three ways that society can accommodate the disabled.

PART 4 One paragraph answer (28 points)

Choose one of the following topics and write a paragraph about it. Use a separate sheet of paper.

1 Equality can be understood in different ways.

2 The United States is becoming more/less egalitarian.

Unit **4** CONTENT QUIZ

PART 1 True/False questions (24 points)

Decide if the following statements are true (T) or false (F).

_____ **1** New technology in the nineteenth century helped factory workers by increasing wages.

_____ **2** Universal education has always been available in the United States.

_____ **3** The founders of the United States believed that people should be judged by what they do, not by where they come from.

_____ **4** The federal government can take away private property if the property will be used for a public purpose.

_____ **5** The rich are getting richer, and the poor are getting poorer in the United States.

_____ **6** Most Americans drive to work.

PART 2 Multiple choice questions (24 points)

Circle the best answer(s) from the choices listed.

1 Factory owners opposed trade unions because
  a they increased competition.
  b they tried to get better pay and better conditions for workers.
  c they opposed new technology.
  d they fought against monopolies.

2 Which of the following is more characteristic of people with only a high school diploma than people with a college degree?
  a They are more likely to vote.
  b They are more likely to be unemployed.
  c They have more children.
  d They tend to be healthier.

3 During the Great Depression, the New Deal
  a provided jobs for the unemployed.
  b increased taxes for the rich.
  c provided health care for the poor.
  d increased educational opportunities for all children.

4 Companies like Wal-Mart are successful because they
  a have more stores than other companies.
  b have low prices and a wide selection of products.
  c provide personal service.
  d are located in large malls.

PART 3 Short answer questions (24 points)

In one or two sentences, write a short answer to each of the following questions.

1 Give two reasons why settlers moved west.

2 Describe three problems that factory workers faced in the nineteenth century.

3 What are two advantages of a college degree?

PART 4 One paragraph answer (28 points)

Choose one of the following topics and write a paragraph about it. Use a separate sheet of paper.

1 Universal education is an important part of a democratic society.

2 Sometimes individual rights conflict with what is best for society.

Unit **5** CONTENT QUIZ

PART 1 True/False questions (24 points)

Decide if the following statements are true (T) or false (F).

_____ **1** Baseball has always been the most popular sport in the United States.

_____ **2** The United States is the leader in cell phone technology.

_____ **3** Americans spend more than 100 billion dollars on fast food every year.

_____ **4** Hip-hop culture originated in poor communities in Africa.

_____ **5** Hollywood movies were an important form of entertainment during the Depression.

_____ **6** It is estimated that a billion people speak English as their first language.

PART 2 Multiple choice questions (24 points)

Circle the best answer from the choices listed.

1 Jazz is significant in American history because it
   a shows the importance of the southern part of the country.
   b encourages individual performance.
   c helped bring blacks and whites together.
   d has roots in the blues.

2 Basketball
   a has its roots in a sport played in England in the mid-nineteenth century.
   b became an Olympic sport after World War II.
   c is the most popular sport in the United States.
   d was invented to provide an indoor activity.

3 English
   a has more nonnative speakers than native speakers.
   b has almost a million speakers.
   c is an official language in more than half the countries in the world.
   d never changes.

4 The Internet is faster, more efficient, and more reliable than earlier forms of communication because it
   a uses telephones.
   b doesn't rely on electricity.
   c occupies a global space.
   d allows information to be sent over many different routes.

PART 3 Short answer questions (24 points)

In one or two sentences, write a short answer to each of the following questions.

1 Why is fast food popular worldwide?

2 Why has hip-hop culture become so popular all over the world?

3 Name one or two advantages of the Internet and one or two disadvantages.

PART 4 One paragraph answer (28 points)

Choose one of the following topics and write a paragraph about it. Use a separate sheet of paper.

1 Access to technology for everyone is important in a democracy.

2 Cultural activities and changes reflect the values of a society.

Unit 1 CONTENT QUIZ ANSWERS

PART 1

F	1
T	2
F	3
F	4
F	5
T	6

PART 2

b	1
d	2
a	3
b	4

PART 3

1 A federalist system of government divides power and responsibility between the central and state governments.

2 In the popular vote, citizens vote directly for their candidate. In the electoral vote for the President, citizens vote indirectly through electors.

3 The purpose of the Bill of Rights is to protect the rights of individuals, especially from any abuse of power by the government.

PART 4

1 The response should discuss the three branches of government, their powers, and the checks by the other branches that limit these powers.

2 The response should include the idea that one person's freedom of speech ends when it causes clear harm to another person. It should include examples of dangerous and libelous speech.

Unit 2 CONTENT QUIZ ANSWERS

PART 1

_T_ 1

_T_ 2

_F_ 3

_F_ 4

_T_ 5

_T_ 6

PART 2

_c_ 1

_d_ 2

_a_ 3

_d_ 4

PART 3

1 Answers should include three of the following factors: new diseases introduced by the Europeans, broken treaties, assimilationist educational policies, and forcible removal of Native Americans from their lands.

2 Answers should include two of the following arguments: drain on government resources, competition for jobs, and dilution of national identity, including language use.

3 Answers should include three of the following groups: slave traders, ship owners, rum producers, cotton farmers, clothing factory owners, and people who bought cotton clothing.

PART 4

1 The response should include the various forms of hostility and violence that immigrants have experienced throughout history. It should include examples from the past, such as the experiences of the Chinese and the Irish, as well as resentment against immigrants today.

2 The response should include the notion that as long as there are dramatic economic differences between the United States and the developing world, illegal immigration will continue. Immigrants will come for better economic opportunities, and the United States will need the cheap labor that they provide.

Unit 3 CONTENT QUIZ ANSWERS

PART 1

T   **1**

F   **2**

T   **3**

F   **4**

T   **5**

T   **6**

PART 2

c   **1**

d   **2**

a   **3**

d   **4**

PART 3

1 Answers should refer to economic profiles and representation in government.

2 Answers should refer to literacy tests, voting taxes, and grandfather laws.

3 Answers can include any of the following: The government can provide assistance in education, transportation, and communication. Businesses can assist by hiring the disabled and providing special equipment necessary for them to do their jobs. Government, business, and public institutions can accommodate the disabled by providing easy access, for example, ramps, elevators, and special parking places.

PART 4

1 The response should include the three interpretations discussed in the text: (1) all people are essentially the same, and therefore, equal; (2) everyone should have equal opportunity and access; and (3) there should be a guarantee of equal outcomes.

2 This response is the most subjective of all of the quiz items so far and will allow the most latitude, but it should include support for the position taken. A "more egalitarian" response should refer to the recent progress in education and economic status by minorities. A "less egalitarian" response should refer to the remaining gap between majority and minority and between rich and poor. The response might include some discussion of the institutional structures that suggest the groups will remain apart with regard to, for example, school funding.

Unit 4 CONTENT QUIZ ANSWERS

PART 1

F 1

F 2

T 3

T 4

T 5

T 6

PART 2

b 1

b 2

a 3

b 4

PART 3

1 The response should include two of the following: Many settlers moved west to find good farmland and to get away from big cities. Many thought of the West as a land of unlimited economic opportunities and resources, such as minerals, forests, and animals. Students may also mention the dream of a freer life in a wilder place than the cities had become, and the search for a place in which social class was even less important.

2 Reasons should include three of the following: Wages were low, there were no benefits, factories were dangerous, and there was a lot of competition for jobs.

3 Advantages include a better chance of finding a good job; higher salaries; the tendency of people with higher education to have better health, have children who also obtain higher education, and be less likely to become unemployed or go to prison.

PART 4

1 The response should include the notion that education in the United States has long been considered society's equalizer. Anyone who gets a good education, no matter what their background, can compete with other Americans in business, government, and in society in general. Only educated citizens can participate fully in the democratic system.

2 The response should refer to the fact that laws and policies that protect and provide for individuals may go against the interests of society as a whole. The response should include historical and current examples of this conflict, for example, eminent domain and affirmative action.

Unit **5** CONTENT QUIZ ANSWERS

PART 1

<u>F</u> **1**

<u>F</u> **2**

<u>T</u> **3**

<u>F</u> **4**

<u>T</u> **5**

<u>T</u> **6**

PART 2

<u>c</u> **1**

<u>d</u> **2**

<u>a</u> **3**

<u>d</u> **4**

PART 3

1 Fast food is fast, convenient, and in many parts of the world, relatively inexpensive. In addition, in the view of many consumers, it is fashionable and tastes good.

2 Hip-hop culture represents and unites young people all over the world, giving them a unifying identity. In addition, many people think hip-hop culture gives a voice to oppressed communities everywhere.

3 The response should include benefits such as broad access to information, the sharing of ideas and information, and the general benefit of bringing people of the world closer together. Drawbacks include access to dangerous ideas and information, the spread of hate speech, and the threats to privacy and private information.

PART 4

1 The response should include the idea that access to ideas and information is an important factor in participating in a democratic system. It gives more people both the knowledge and the power to make their ideas a part of the democratic process.

2 The response should include, but should not be limited to, such topics from the texts as the connections between music and social justice; between the popularity of cars and the yearning for freedom and independence; between the growth of the fast-food industry and the pace of life today; or between the Internet and today's desire for immediate connections and responses. This topic also provides an opportunity for students to write more from their own experiences.